ON REREADING CHAUCER

On Rereading Chaucer

By

Howard Rollin Patch

CAMBRIDGE, MASSACHUSETTS
HARVARD UNIVERSITY PRESS
1959

Third Printing

DISTRIBUTED IN GREAT BRITAIN BY

OXFORD UNIVERSITY PRESS, LONDON

PRINTED AT THE HARVARD UNIVERSITY PRINTING OFFICE

CAMBRIDGE, MASSACHUSETTS, U.S.A.

TO MY SISTERS
EMILY AND ETHEL

Although his lyfe be queynt, the resemblaunce
Of him hath in me so fressh lyflynesse,
That, to putte othir men in remembraunce
Of his persone, I have heere his lyknesse
Do make, to this ende in sothfastnesse,
    That thei that have of him lest thought and mynde,
    By this peynture may ageyn him fynde.

THOMAS HOCCLEVE, *The Regement of Princes*

PREFACE

In the present set of essays I attempt to give expression to some of the ideas I have had over the years about Chaucer's literary works. It may be noted that what I have here put down has occurred to me "on rereading Chaucer," and, I may now add, after rereading him many times. Even so I imagine some friendly enemy in the field of criticism taking a look at my pages and saying, "Let him read the poet once again!" The privilege happily remains for all of us. Many of my observations still remain tentative, and I may say that I am in favor of admitting tentative judgments, since they will encourage other readers to offer their differing views, the stimulation of disagreement will arise, and everyone will turn to the poet himself to confirm some statements or to refute others.

There is a certain lack of unity in this book, as I am well aware. In general my remarks are strung together on the theme of Chaucer's humor, but I have not hesitated to wander off to deal with some other subject if it seemed profitable for discussion. Moreover I have not defined my terms closely, and I have not been systematic enough to let the reader know fully what I mean by the humorous, the comic, the satiric. I suppose I have felt justified in assuming that most readers would have a fair idea of what I was driving at; and I have feared that if anyone got too close to my meaning he might be disposed to controversy. For the moment I have no objection to adopting George Meredith's definitions, in what has been attacked as a very unsystematic essay, where he gives his explanation as follows: "The comic, which is the perceptive, is the governing spirit, awakening and giving aim to these powers of laughter, but it is not to be confounded with them; it enfolds a thinner form of them, differing from satire in not sharply driving into the quivering sensibilities, and from humor in not comforting them and tucking them up, or indicating a broader than the range of this bustling world to them." Incidentally this note on the "comforting" power of humor might be broadened to include its general yield of the resources of strength. It is a healthy sense.

Meredith's own remarks on Chaucer are provocative. In speaking of the *Misanthrope* and *Tartuffe* he observes: "They quicken the mind through laughter, from coming out of the mind. . . ." But earlier he has remarked: "The Comic Spirit is not hostile to the sweetest songfully poetic. Chaucer bubbles with it; Shakespeare overflows; there is a mild moon's ray of it (pale with super-refinement through distance from our flesh and blood planet) in *Comus*." Now some of this is apt enough. I recommend to students of Milton the reflections on the quality of his mirth. I am aware also that there is a nice indication here of the constant and spontaneous element in the flow of what the other two poets offer. But I cannot help a slight suspicion that Meredith was hardly aware of the extent to which Chaucer's mind (let alone Shakespeare's) functioned. What he says has the manner that comes from reading too much of a certain type of comment on Chaucer, the sort that dwells on his descriptions of Spring and the way the daisy looks in the fields. Take for instance what Mr. Llewelyn Powys sets forth: "Daisies! it was not for nothing that Chaucer selected that brave, contented, little English flower to be his especial favourite." Indeed it was not for nothing: the sophisticated, allegorical purpose of the poet's use of this item can be found fully explained in any handbook. But there is little evidence that Chaucer bubbled. His poetry, I think, has not worked in that way, even if it springs ultimately from a wine cellar; nor do I find his exhilaration always effervescent. His humor is as quiet, although as active and intense, as sunlight. It is natural, not produced. A stream may bubble, but chiefly because of its interruptions. Chaucer's humor is less a flow of good spirits than an attitude of mind: "a way of thinking, an attitude to life," as M. Cazamian describes it. Or rather it comes from the light of the man's whole personality.

Perhaps it is important nowadays to ask whether there is anything peculiarly national in Chaucer's variety of humor. M. Cazamian would claim something of his "slyness" for France and French influence. On the other hand, I am ready to see a German sense of grotesquery in such passages as his descriptions of the Miller, the Summoner, and the Cook, which commend themselves to the art of a Dürer. But this problem I leave to others. Humor is in part an international possession, and it is also, I hope, a universal solvent.

But did he ever suspend for a time the operation of this important sense? Some readers may find that he did in the story of Constance, or in that of Virginia, or even in the *Prioress's Tale*. In such cases I hardly think it was held in abeyance; it was simply not apropos, as it was not in the *Par-*

son's Tale. There is no evidence of that loss of a sense of proportion in these stories which we might expect to find if humor is deliberately withheld. Stories like monologues vary in content, and moods vary in color. Chaucer's luck in discovering most of his pilgrims at a special moment of self-revelation has been noticed by a better critic elsewhere, and such performances as those by the Pardoner and the Wife of Bath and the Canon's Yeoman compensate for any suspected thinness in other narratives on the pilgrimage. With regard to the poet's humor, however, we may say that it is never presumptuously forward. In using it Chaucer does not strike a professional pose.

The text used in the present study is that of *The Complete Works of Geoffrey Chaucer* (Boston: Houghton Mifflin, 1933), edited by Professor F. N. Robinson. It is quoted here by permission of the publishers. For the few passages from Shakespeare I have used Professor Kittredge's edition, published by Ginn and Company in 1936. For the passages quoted (with slight modification) from Mr. F. S. Ellis's translation of the *Roman de la Rose* I am indebted to E. P. Dutton & Company for permission to use the edition published in the Temple Classics.

Three of the essays in this book have appeared before. "Troilus on Determinism" was published in *Speculum*, VI (1931), 225–243; "Chaucer and the Common People" was printed in the *Journal of English and Germanic Philology*, XXIX (1930), 376–384; and "Chaucer and Medieval Romance" was included in the *Essays in Memory of Barrett Wendell*, pp. 95–108. For permission to use this material again (in which I have made a very few unimportant changes and omitted documentation) I am grateful to the Editors of these respective publications and to the Harvard University Press. For reading most of my manuscript and for suggesting minor alterations I am also under obligation to Professor George L. Kittredge, Sir Herbert Grierson, President William A. Neilson of Smith College, and Professor Charles J. Hill. There are other debts that should be noticed. If at times my criticism shows insight, I owe the achievement, at least in part, to Dr. Neilson, an inspiring teacher and a tolerant friend, and to Professor Kittredge, who has been a master to many of us. Old debts of the same sort, long left without acknowledgment, are those to Professor John Muirheid, Professor Milton H. Turk, and Professor Philip B. Goetz. For points in the psychological study of some of the characters I am indebted to my friends Dr. Thaddeus H. Ames and Professor William S. Taylor.

A special word of gratitude, however, should go to my companion of many years, my wife, who now repudiates the adjective "patient" but who in encouraging me to the performance of this task and in seeing it through has been "evere in oon ylike sad and kynde."

H. R. P.

Northampton, Massachusetts
January, 1939

CONTENTS

ON REREADING CHAUCER

Chapter I

THE IDEA OF HUMOR

IN A CLASSIC and nowadays generally unread essay, James Russell Lowell indicated an essential quality in Geoffrey Chaucer when he spoke of him as "healthy." To this he added the word "hearty," which is undoubtedly accurate for certain of Chaucer's moods, although I am not quite so sure of its further application. The health of the poet's spirit is pervasive in all his works, which exhibit nothing that from any point of view may be called morbid, however much they may show stretches arid to modern taste or passages offensive to the excessively puritanical. No strains from the music of the Dance of Death, which pleased certain ears in the Middle Ages and the Renaissance, no rarefied religiosity or unworldly melancholy mar his lines. As we cannot say of Swift or Pope or Sterne, no rancor poisons the spring of his genius; he has less acerbity than Dryden, and unlike many writers he does not pause in his verse for intervals of bad temper. His peculiar trait may perhaps be described by the allied expression "sanity." "Whether Chaucer saw life whole, I do not know," writes Professor Kittredge. "One thing I know — he saw it steadily."

Dryden had the characteristic in mind when he referred to the poet's "good sense." But what I am now moved to inquire is whether it might not equally well be called "good humor." Contrasting him with Dante, whose satire is "like a blast of the divine wrath," Lowell goes on to say that Chaucer's "is genial with the broad sunshine of humor, into which the victims walk forth with a delightful unconcern, laying aside of themselves the disguises that seem to make them uncomfortably warm, till they have made a thorough betrayal of themselves so unconsciously that we almost pity while we laugh." All this applies well enough to writings in this vein, but what about his poetry and prose where satiric purpose seems to be mainly absent? Do we find there the light of the same healthy spirit playing upon the narrative and illuminating its significance? Or perhaps it does not busy itself with significance at all, but simply affords the pleasure that health and humor in themselves are likely to create. Is Chaucer's quality the same thing as sanity after all, in the sense that the term implies the possession of wisdom? And is the humor he shows anything more than the symptom of physical well-being, expressing itself through the instinct of play, restraining him, it may well be, from piercing into those depths of understanding where the tragic note must be heard and high seriousness is perpetually at home?

With some interest in such problems as these I have been reading Chaucer's works for many years, mindful of the advice of a great critic that one must live in the poet's company before one ventures to think one at least partly understands him. Humor there is almost everywhere in his works; I have no doubt of that. But when it comes to a demonstration of the point, the task is supremely difficult. Readers who perceive none here or there will always urge that it is not present, that we are reading things into lines that were meant to be taken at their face value, and doubtless that we are moved by some dark purpose to uncover irony or mirth where none was intended. Concerning the perception of values there can never be argument. Chaucer himself must have found the reader who is lacking in humor particularly hard to manage. Insight into the matter of humor is in any case a delicate faculty, and as it varies from one individual to another so it has differed in intensity from one century to another. In the long history of the appreciation of Chaucer's poetry, as it is spread before us in Miss Spurgeon's *Five Hundred Years of Chaucer Criticism and Allusion*, one may see that understanding of this special feature has been slow in developing. "It is not . . . until well on in the nineteenth century," Miss Spurgeon observes, "not indeed until Leigh Hunt wrote on it in 1846, that Chaucer's humour seems to have met with any adequate recognition." Francis Beaumont, it is true, found the poet "the verie life it selfe of all mirth and pleasant writing," a comment I like to remember. But Samuel Johnson thought the "tale of *The Cock*" "hardly worth revival," and another eighteenth-century writer regarded it as "foolish, if not worse." They must have assumed, as Addison had written:

> . . . Age has rusted what the *Poet* writ
> Worn out his Language, and obscur'd his Wit:
> In vain he jests in his unpolish'd strain
> And tries to make his Readers laugh in vain.

The *Parliament of Fowls* could survive, I suppose, as a "poet's poem," so to speak; the *Troilus* and the *Knight's Tale* could stand on their feet as straight narrative. Even to-day there are readers who find the *House of Fame* dull.

Not only in critical writing but in the modernizations one can see the failure to catch the particular flavor of Chaucer's humor. I am not concerned to prove this point, but I may illustrate it by a reference to one of the best modern renderings, written by a poet with exceptional insight. Take the story of Midas in the *Wife of Bath's Tale* and in Dryden's rendering. For my purpose I shall quote only the ending, first as it is in Chaucer. The wife of Midas thus tells her secret:

> "Biwreye me nat, thou water, with thy soun,"
> Quod she; "to thee I telle it and namo;
> Myn housbonde hath longe asses erys two!
> Now is myn herte al hool, now is it oute.
> I myghte no lenger kepe it, out of doute."
>
> D. 974–978.

And thus it is rendered by Dryden:

> "To thee alone, O lake," she said, "I tell
> (And, as thy queen, command thee to conceal,)
> Beneath his locks the king my husband wears
> A goodly royal pair of ass's ears:
> Now I have eas'd my bosom of the pain,
> Til the next longing fit return again!"
>
> 195–200.

Some humor inevitably remains, of course. But the compactness within the line, the pat rhymes, the gasp of relief in the repeated "now," are all missing. Thus in the seventeenth century one had to polish the rough diamond. So Alexander Pope changed what he took from the *House of Fame* for his *Temple*. As Thomas Campbell wrote, "Much of Chaucer's fantastic matter has been judiciously omitted. . . . In Pope, the philosophy of fame comes with much more propriety from the poet himself than from the beak of a talkative eagle." How ill we could spare the bird despite the gain in propriety! With Pope the man of great authority who comes in at the end challenges the dreamer, who concludes the poem with an aspiration:

> "Then teach me, Heav'n! to scorn the guilty bays;
> Drive from my breast that wretched lust of praise;
> Unblemish'd let me live or die unknown;
> Oh, grant an honest fame, or grant me none!"
>
> 521–524.

The point is open to dispute, but I am strongly of the opinion that Chaucer's poem, if it was ever completed, did not end that way.

But the question doubtless rises as to what we mean by humor. This we must make clear if ever we are to examine instances in the poet's works and relate our observations to a consideration of his healthy spirit and good sense. It is, I think, based on a sense of incongruity, probably between the transitory and the permanent. This is the essence of Bergson's definition, in the clash he envisages between the mechanical or static and the changing and living. When a man stumbles he may offer a comic appearance; the humor of the episode lies in the incongruity between his normal self as a properly functioning man and the instant interruption of his procedure. We hardly need to decide whether the man is for the moment the victim of the mechanical, or whether such incidents are the result of the play of unreasoning force, which is the evil spirit in Plato's cosmogony. One thing is certain, the effect of the incongruity can hardly be disastrous or humor is replaced by tragic irony. Also it may be insisted that no feeling of superiority is required in the onlooker (though it may indeed be present); humor is allied to the spirit of play. Fundamentally no doubt the sense of incongruity is based on detachment — perhaps even an awareness of escape — and a sense of proportion; for by a sense of proportion we imply, I think, some insight into the distinction between the transitory and the permanent. By permanent, I hasten to say, we need not mean everlasting or eternal, only that which endures. And the onlooker who perceives the humor of a situation may not only be guiltless of all feeling of superiority but see in a comic episode implications that include appeals to something close to pity and terror. Remember, Onlooker, you may stumble too!

But we need not attempt to go deeply into this problem. My purpose here is not primarily philosophical or systematic. I offer these remarks tentatively as I do the observations that follow in the succeeding chapters. We can take pleasure in noticing what seems to fall into the class of what is humorous and make many other observations as well. For my hope is really by comment and discussion to reveal more of the meaning of Chaucer than has been perceived hitherto. I have even the desire to find out something more of what the poet himself was like, and certain of the conditions that lay behind the composition of some of his works. In the process I believe there will appear now and then new evidence to support Lowell's dictum, but I am far from intending to write a discourse on the single theme of humor. Much may be turned up in any search by an indirect approach, and, in an age when readers inevitably differ on fundamentals aesthetic as well as philosophical, impressionistic criticism is at times our only resource.

Let me not seem, however, to discount a scholarly approach to the subject. Shooting feathered arrows of thought here and there into problems undoubtedly reveals much that is missed by a judicious and logical procedure. But too much has been made of the failure of the scientific method in the field of aesthetics. Especially in the case of writers living in another age than ours, when the language was different and the whole attitude toward writing was on another basis, it is the scholar who has spent long hours training himself in a real sense for Middle English meanings, who has watched the intricacy of borrowing — to-day we might mistakenly say pilfering — by one poet from another in the process of composition, it is he who can perceive subtle implications in the use of material and who now and then must lead the way in criticism. This is not to maintain that he will always be right in his judgments, but that he has on one side at least a better chance of being right. He knows, let us say, how Deschamps used a theme in one of his works, and thus he catches overtones when he finds Chaucer putting the same ideas in a very different context. In a masterly way Professor Lowes showed the connotation of the phrases in the description of the Prioress which the English poet took from the *Roman de la Rose* and the poetry of Courtly Love. Let me quote from his remarks regarding her smile "simple and coy": "There, in the second line, is struck the keynote of the description. The convention didn't belong to the nun at all, as nun. To every one of Chaucer's readers its distinctly earthly rather than heavenly flavor was unmistakable."

Moreover the real student will not be misled by modern developments of the word "coy" into thinking that it suggests the affectedly demure.

Such an obvious instance of the scholar's advantage is necessary to cite in view of the fact that he is often suspect the moment he steps out of his rôle as the hunter of literary sources or the cataloguer of grammatical forms. It was by Mr. Lowes's tireless pursuit of the phrase "simple and coy" in line after line of poetry that he perceived its background and its redolent association. In a fashion almost parallel Mr. Kittredge's study of the *Book of the Duchess* and its French sources enabled him to see that it is French to the fingertips and at the same time highly original: "For Chaucer uses his borrowings with the power of a master, and nowhere in the poem does his originality appear more strikingly than in the description of the Duchess Blanche, — the very place where his indebtedness is most conspicuous." Now we may recall that this description is presumably a portrait and that in this collection, mostly of borrowed lines, fourteenth-century readers could see the lady's actual features. It is an astounding fact, but one that only the scholar could have made clear. Of the poem Mr. Kittredge further remarks: "Never was there a more conventional situation — a dream, a paradise of trees and flowers and birds, a lamenting lover, an incomparable lady. We who wander through the middle ages have seen and heard it all a hundred times." Yes, we may reflect, but it took much thoughtful wandering before these observations could be made. It signifies all the more that years of such study have preceded the conclusions here and elsewhere enunciated in Mr. Kittredge's essay, as he restores the poem to its proper place of dignity in criticism. He is able to detect the conventional by comparison with other poetry of the kind, and he can also indicate in what way "the conventions are [here] vitalized."

One reason why Lowell's essay is to-day commonly unread is that, despite its own delightful quality of freshness, a quality it has assimilated from Chaucer, much of it has passed into common property and is no longer new. Another reason is that in certain points it seems mistaken, as when Lowell observed, ". . . for I think it a great mistake to attribute to [Chaucer] any properly dramatic power, as some have done." But certainly still another reason is that its scholarship is out of date. I am reminded of William Hazlitt's error as he writes: "One of the finest parts of Chaucer is of this mixed kind. It is the beginning of the Flower and the Leaf, where he describes the delight of that young beauty, shrouded in her bower, and listening, in the morning of the year, to the singing of the nightingale. . . ." But we now know that he did not write the *Flower and the Leaf*. Isaac Disraeli quotes with approval the statement that "of all poets, Chaucer seems to have been fondest of the singing of birds." But first we must know whether the lines attributed to him about birds are genuinely his. And, if so, did he coldly take them over for reasons that have little to do with their song? For they are found in almost countless passages describing nature; as a student, who has investigated medieval accounts of the seasons, laments: ". . . one cannot hope to be exhaustive when one deals with centuries of 'singing birds.'" The critic is dependent on the scholar·and facts must be tested before inferences are made. Thus Disraeli writes: "It

was behind the bars of a gloomy window in the Tower . . .
that Chaucer, recent from exile and sore from persecution,
was reminded of a work popular in those days, and which
had been composed in a dungeon, — 'The Consolations of
Philosophy,' by Boethius. . . . He composed his 'Testament
of Love,' substituting for the severity of an abstract being
the more genial inspiration of love itself." But, again, we
are now quite certain that this work was not his, and the
discovery of its true authorship was made in time for
Lowell to say: "We are thankful that Chaucer's shoulders
are finally discharged of that weary load, 'The Testament
of Love.' "

But it would be churlish not to recognize the gifts of the
critic and merely to list examples of this kind. I simply want
to urge that the most valid criticism of at least the older poets
will come, to be sure, from one who has an insight into
aesthetic values but also from one who has gone through
some of the process followed by the scholar. If this provision
is allowed, impressionistic criticism is still possible on its own
terms. Yet it will be somewhat affected in its procedure; for
it should take account not only of the impression a work of
art makes on its modern readers but of that which it was
intended to make on readers at any time, and here again
scholarship will have something to say. Indeed the result will
be similar to judicial criticism if the judgments, the prejudices,
the principles of the writer, are examined with reference to
what he does. While the reader may not share the philosophy of the poet, he must include it in his consideration of
artistic values, or he will miss important .elements in that
emotional pattern which the poet has designed. If he finds

fault with the philosophy because it is shallow, he may seem
to have left the realm of aesthetic criticism; but his aim quite
justly may be to show its weakness in comparison with some
other which would have a richer emotional and thus artistic
content. For example, he may complain if a writer is so
romantic as to set forth only what is remote from life and
experience, since an art so little realistic is not the one to
move the reader most profoundly in terms of his own experience. If the critic, following Longinus, searches for the
"great thoughts" which are the mark of the sublime, he
must at some time ponder over the problem of what char-
acterizes the greatness of the thought.

But when a critic thus takes account of something other
than mere texture and pigment, if he drags in philosophy and
morals, he incurs the risk at once of being denounced as
academic. He will probably slip at times into the use of
technical expressions. He may at times be systematic and
even conscientious. He can reply, of course, that in all such
aberrations his purpose is no worse than to illuminate and
reveal, but even then he will be regarded with distrust. The
Host on the pilgrimage to Canterbury felt he must warn the
Clerk:

> "Youre termes, youre colours, and youre figures,
> Keepe hem in stoor til so be that ye endite
> Heigh style, as whan that men to kynges write."
>   E. 16–18.

I think there is a shot here at all fine writing. The only obvious remedy is to avoid the logic of the monograph, and to
adopt a method less direct and more casual. This will be an

advantage to anyone who sets out to investigate the poet's humor; for such a task involves special difficulties of its own. In being systematic about that a scholar can be far too funny for what he is trying to do, without uncovering the full humor of the original. It is hard to prove that at least a smile is hidden where none has been seen before. It is safer to disclaim the intention of dealing with the subject at all, or at any rate to make it only a subordinate consideration.

I still admire Professor Saintsbury's comments on certain aspects of this "all-pervading" quality in Chaucer. It is one, he quickly and I think cautiously adds, "which some, even of those who enjoy it heartily and extol it generously, do not quite invariably seem to comprehend." He alludes to some readers who seem "destitute of the sense itself." This humor, he continues, " 'works i' the earth so fast' that you never can tell at what moment it will find utterance. . . . It is by no means certain that in [Chaucer's] displays of learning he is not mocking or parodying others as well as relieving himself. It is by no means certain that, seriously as we know him to have been interested in astronomy, his frequent astronomical or astrological lucubrations are not partly ironical." "His good humour is even more pervading. It gives a memorable distinction of kindliness between *The Wife of Bath's Prologue* and the brilliant following of it by Dunbar in *The Tua Mariit Wemen and the Wedo*; and it even separates Chaucer from such later humorists as Addison and Jane Austen, who, though never savage, can be politely cruel. Cruelty and Chaucer are absolute strangers. . . ." Well, in the sense that Addison and Jane Austen showed their finesse, I am not so sure whether Chaucer's satire was any less mordant. What about the Pardoner and the Merchant in their own stories? But I am now chiefly interested in Mr. Saintsbury's fear that not all readers will find the quality of humor where he does, and that he must expound it for the unseeing. This I fancy is a hopeless undertaking; all that can be done is for those who agree in perceiving it here and there to rejoice together. Disquisitions must be left for more serious business.

Some years ago, when the date of the poet's birth was much discussed, passages in his works which happen to refer to his age were brought forward as evidence that when he wrote a certain poem he was so and so many years old. Thus in the *House of Fame* we read the challenge of the talkative eagle:

> "Wilt thou lere of sterres aught?"
> "Nay, certeynly," quod y, "ryght naught."
> "And why?" "For y am now to old."
> 993–995.

And critics who dated the poem not later than 1386, and perhaps ten years earlier, asked themselves whether the poet if born as late as 1340 or 1346 could have regarded himself as too old at forty-six (or less) to hear something about astronomy. The medieval attitude toward age was studied, and parallels adduced to prove that in those days a man was regarded as old from forty on. But perhaps this poem was written when Chaucer was much younger than that — even at the age of thirty-five, at the prime of life the poet would say and "nel mezzo del cammin di nostra vita" others might urge. Even then there would be point; for in his reply the eagle's victim is only trying to shut off the long edifying discourse to which he has had to listen. And the bird shows his disappointment when he goes on:

> "Elles I wolde the have told,"
> Quod he, "the sterres names, lo,
> And al the hevenes sygnes therto,
> And which they ben." "No fors," quod y.
>   996–999.

The eagle manages to accomplish some of this all the same, and Chaucer cannot stop him entirely. The bird shows the pride in his learning that the Canon's Yeoman feels in his knowledge of alchemy, and pours it out with a similar zest. There is no reason at all to look for evidence of the poet's age here unless we choose to miss another point. But there is reason here to suspect that Chaucer saw the humor of a display of this kind, just as he did in the case of Chantecler and Pertelote. While it is difficult to prove this interpretation, it is none the less important not to miss it lest we suppose that the poet wore his own learning simply as a badge of honor.

But the skeptical may well ask why, if humor was so long in coming to its fruition, as we infer from Miss Spurgeon's survey of Chaucer criticism, there is any likelihood that it flourished or was understood in the fourteenth century. Would the poet, no matter how well endowed himself with this faculty, write in terms which his audience or readers of his own time could not possibly appreciate or grasp? Yet there is no possible doubt that humor, irony, wit, and satire were widely understood and relished in the Middle Ages. The animal epics show it; the student songs have now one, now another of these qualities; the development of comedy leading to the *Second Shepherds' Play* of the Towneley Cycle proves the point; wit and sometimes even humor touch the allegories of the Court of Love, as, for instance, in the Church service of the birds in Jean de Condé's *Messe des Oisiaus*. Chaucer's contemporaries, Gower and Lydgate, were not strong in this type of appeal, that is certain; but there is a touch in the *Tale of Florent* and something more in *Bycorne and Chichevache*. Chaucer got some of his material in this vein from Deschamps. His Envoys to Scogan and to Bukton and to Sir Philip la Vache show that there were some people to enjoy his subtlety. I think his reference to Gower in the Introduction to the *Man of Law's Tale*, when he says that he himself never wrote of Canacee (of such cursed stories he says fie!), and his allusion to moral Gower at the end of the *Troilus*, were both meant to be humorous (or something like it) for others than just himself. He makes fun of others as he makes fun of himself, and he gives every impression that his fun was meant to be shared. How high the general average of humor was in the period he wrote, it is hardly possible to determine here. Yet, considering the elements in Chaucer's works which are generally accepted as humorous in purpose, we may say that the poet found a contemporary spirit that prompted him to the full expression of this talent, and an assurance in his world that his fullest inspiration in this sort of writing would meet a response.

It remains to inquire whether the highest type of appeal can ever be made in writing of this sort. Even to-day there are readers who regard humor as trivial, as if comedy must always be an interlude, and mirth a little lower than the

dignity of the angels; we have it on high authority that jesting and foolish talking are sometimes inconvenient. Chaucer
can reach the heights in realism, yes, and, if he can step ele-
gantly enough, in the romantic; but can the sublime be
achieved through humor? To answer this question at once we
have only to recall the great examples. I have said that humor
implies a sense of harmless incongruity between the transitory and the permanent, and this whatever its overtones is
found in the scene of the knocking at the gate in *Macbeth*.
For many this scene long had nothing better than the meaning of the irrelevant. But in a subtle way that is its very point.
De Quincey taught criticism its deeper meaning, the incongruity lodged in the porter's silly speech contrasted with the
knocking of a world demanding admittance to tragedy.
While the episode as a whole has its own grim irony, the
porter's speech is harmless enough; by its use the humor is
lifted to sublimity. Or if it be maintained that by this process
the humor is transmuted into something else, there is always
the scene of Falstaff and Hal, where the Prince issues his
challenge. The Hostess has quoted the rascal's boast that the
Prince owes him a thousand pounds:

> *Prince.* Sirrah, do I owe you a thousand pound?
> *Falstaff.* A thousand pound, Hal? A million!
> Thy love is worth a million; thou owest me thy love.
> *I Henry the Fourth*, III, iii, 153–157.

Wit there is here in the quick turn, no doubt, and pathos as
well, but they serve the dominant humor. It is to this expression of love between the two great characters that the
later rebuke emotionally points back, when Hal says: "I

know thee not, old man. Fall to thy prayers." (*II Henry the Fourth*, V, v, 51.)

In fact, I find that the sublime may be achieved in humor in various ways. In such illustrations as those just considered it is mainly in terms of human character. The same is true with *Don Quixote* perhaps; together with wit this is what we find in most satiric writing. The weaknesses or the deeps of human nature are made visible, and the operation is effected with less pain than with tragedy. The range of opportunity, all the way from grossness to the intellectual laughter of high comedy, follows the infinite variety of human nature itself. But there is another kind of sublimity in humor, which is familiar with authors who put the emphasis elsewhere. I find it in Molière, who is witty and ironic and also humorous, as in the famous scene when Monsieur Jourdain is provoked to observe that his opponent does not fence according to the rules: ". . . tu me pousses en tierce avant que de pousser en quarte, et tu n'as pas la patience que je pare." (*Le Bourgeois Gentilhomme*, III, iii.) I find it even more where Mme. Jourdain rebukes her husband for cultivating the nobility, and he replies: "Lors que je hante la noblesse, je fais paroistre mon jugement; et cela est plus beau que de hanter vostre bourgeoisie." Here, I think, we find the dramatist likes his leading character for the moment. But the predominating interest of Molière, I think, is less in the values of human nature which he displays than in the situations and indeed the forces that serve to expose them. This possibly is just another way of saying that as an artist he seeks to produce his effect chiefly in his design; he cares more about the pattern than the elements of emotion and human character that compose it. Unlike Shakespeare, who in Falstaff shows many kinds of traits, Molière strings his characteristics on one thread: the avaricious, the hypocrite, and so on. The universality implicit in this concern is a step removed from that which has to do with the general significance of human nature itself; it deals rather with elements in some kind of cosmic plan that discovers human beings to one another or to themselves.

There is, however, at least another kind of sublime humor, and this is more difficult to describe. It is, I believe, the particular quality of the poet whose imagination at once expresses itself symbolically, in a rich profusion of figures of speech dramatically personified or set forth in allegory because literal statement is inadequate. Its stuff, of course, is ultimately human nature and ordinary experience, but transformed into poetry by the intensity of the artist's insight into abstract meanings. This may be found in Aristophanes, in *The Frogs* for example; it also appears in Bottom's translation in *A Midsummer Night's Dream*. It furnishes exquisite notes to *The Tempest* in the person of Caliban as well as in that of Ariel; the whole play, in fact, may be said to be on this level. I can imagine the claim made with good reason that in humor of this type there is something mystical; occasionally its overtones are without doubt celestial. But the mystical may also be present in that of the first and second types. Sufficient belief in the magnificence of human nature (apart entirely from the problem of whether it is fallen from grace, which is another matter) will radiate this quality in humor of the first type. In Molière's comedy the power of life to reveal implies something of almost the same illumination.

But perhaps I must revert to the question whether it is the humor in the instances I have cited which is in itself exalted. The argument on that score I am afraid must depend on the extent to which the reader feels its power. Arnold could not find high seriousness in Chaucer. He has been answered with references to the Epilogue of the *Troilus*, but another critic has shrewdly pointed to part of the speech of the Wife of Bath about herself. Let me quote it:

> But, Lord Crist! whan that it remembreth me
> Upon my yowthe, and on my jolitee,
> It tikleth me aboute myn herte roote.
> Unto this day it dooth myn herte boote
> That I have had my world as in my tyme.
> But age, allas! that al wole envenyme,
> Hath me biraft my beautee and my pith.
> Lat go, farewel! the devel go therwith!
> The flour is goon, ther is namoore to telle;
> The bren, as I best kan, now moste I selle;
> But yet to be right myrie wol I fonde.
> Now wol I tellen of my fourthe housbonde.
>   D. 469–480.

"The positive quality of such a passage as this," wrote Professor Neilson, "its vividness, its zest, its penetration to the very marrow of life, and the informing of every phrase and accent with vital energy, have much more to do with the production of a highly exalted poetic enjoyment than seriousness of treatment or theme." No, sublimity is not a matter of solemnity but rather of vitality, of life itself in its fullness and with all the disturbing implications that accompany it. Religious pictures may or may not show it in the greatest abundance; it may appear also in Rembrandt, or, say, in the smiling cavalier of Franz Hals.

So far in the discussion I have used the word "humor" in the modern sense without apology. But some student, who remembers the old physiology with its humors, or its temperaments based on one or another of these, and who is aware of the sense of the word in the title of certain of Jonson's plays, may reproach me with ambiguity. It is now relevant to point out how this expression, when it assumed anything like the modern meaning, had special reference to human character. One probably thinks of the old use of the term when one reads again the description of the Canterbury pilgrims, although immediately their richness of temperament, their power to escape classification in this way, will strike the analyst. A sense of the incongruity in certain elements of human nature is, I suspect, the first and most elementary form of humor among the types that I have been discussing. The second and third types are more sophisticated, perhaps the production of a fuller insight into life, perhaps only that of a greater creative power of expression. The first, few would deny, is often found in Chaucer. Commenting on the more earthy passages in the *Canterbury Tales*, Mr. de Selincourt suggests "that if such things are comic they are only comic from a sense of incongruity, and that their whole humour depends ultimately upon that ideal which they seem to travesty or to outrage," and further ". . . the Wife of Bath's philosophy of life is only amusing to you in so far as you do not share it." Here the perception of the distinction between the transitory and the permanent is plain enough, and the suggestion has its value. But I

would urge that the humor consists less in the outraged ideal
than in the spectacle of human nature as we know it and in
part share it. We do not feel the humor of these pilgrims in
so far as they are unlike us; on the contrary we have a bond
in our common weaknesses. This is not to say, I hasten to
add, that these weaknesses, though they make the whole
world kin, must in every way or at all times possess us. But
I think we enter most fully into the play when we know
them from experience, and when we feel perhaps a kind of
personal release we have longed for in the blunder or exposure or slip of someone besides ourselves. Does not Freud
suggest something of the sort in his explanation of laughter?
There can be no doubt that what Chaucer represents is an
assortment of traits characteristic of mankind at large.

But does he show any other sort of humor? As the question is put I find the shadow of academic halls upon me,
and I confess it irks me and hampers speech. I cannot list
the types of humor again and catalogue instances. Some day
when the technique of science has revealed all the truth
available in literature, this will be done. All possible types
of humor will be set down and the examples subjoined in
proper and graded order, and one can then turn to the special
case one desires or see in the graphical outline appended the
general trend of development. We shall be able to prove
perhaps that when Chaucer left the Custom House his
humor increased for a season, or again that the daily pitcher
of wine awarded to him served more to sadden than to cheer.
On the other hand, it may be evident that when his verse was
at its merriest he was most bored with life. But I cannot offer
a contribution to such a study except by the attempt to make

his meaning clearer or to suggest certain qualities in his nature or to say what I suppose to be his intention here and there. If these remarks are modified by readers who come closer to that great and pleasant genius, I can only be the happier. For, as everyone will agree, it is more important to know what Chaucer meant than it is to enjoy what the critic says.

Chapter II

THE COURT OF LOVE

JOHN OF GAUNT, Duke of Lancaster, was a great knight. In his campaigns in France and Spain he showed himself a most valiant warrior; apparently he liked a good fight if the end were crowned with glory. Counselor to young Richard and dignified with certain royal claims of his own, he was fitted by temperament to succeed to the English throne, although Fate and his own right arm gave him only the picturesque eminence of being King of Castile through marriage. The startling contrasts of his life, his defense of Wycliffe when the great Lollard was hounded by enemies and his repudiation of the man when the heretical nature of Lollardry was made clear, his constant sympathy with the poor and the response of hatred from the great throng of rebels who burned the Savoy, his ambition not without its touch of swashbuckling and his humble obedience to the Church, all commend themselves to the modern biographer with a taste for ironies. At one period married to the saintly Constance and beginning every day with Mass, the Duke nevertheless managed an amour with his children's governess, Katharine Swynford, and kept his faith in his own fashion, as we can see when two years after the death of Constance he married his mistress and legitimized their children. "Sage et imaginatif" is the way Froissart described him. We can put it in a medieval manner by saying that like

Roland he was "proz" and like Oliver "sages," with the energy of Godfrey de Bouillon and the power of Charlemagne.

But if there are inconsistencies in his life they suit the pageantry of fourteenth-century England, which men called "merry" despite the Black Death and the sufferings and revolt of the peasants, when treatises on Vice and Virtue and social documents like *Piers Plowman* were read, and yet the elegances of French manners and French poetry on themes of the Court of Love were familiar. The life of the time affords God's plenty; the corrupt as well as the pious walk together on the road to Canterbury for reasons all their own. If the earthly pilgrimage arrives at holiness, there is much to be said along the way. Nationalism, individualism of all kinds, are in the air, and there is gusto in everybody when new things are afoot, especially when the ideas thus embodied spell risk. But the literature of the period is in the main simple and even conventional; the expression even of passion still follows old patterns. The sentiment and realism of Courtly Love dominated the vogue, borrowing force from Ovid and from the *Roman de la Rose*, which, though a century old, continued to fascinate readers, while its pretty design was often imitated.

Of all the chapters of John of Gaunt's history which one would like to know fully, the most appealing perhaps is the story of his love affair with his first wife, Blanche. Here was true romance. It lasted only ten years; but from the time when the Duke made arrangements for the Masses for her soul (the entries are found all through his Register) until the day his will directed that his body should lie in St Paul's

close to his lady's remains ("juxte ma treschere jadys com-
paigne Blanch"), the evidence of his undying devotion —
despite other attachments — is ample enough. In his youth
no doubt he had been a "great lover and a lusty bachelor";
here was the object of his first adoration. When Queen
Philippa and the Duchess Blanche were fatally stricken, the
Duke was abroad, and the bitter news greeted him on his
return from Picardy. All glad thoughts were henceforth
turned to sadness. Which of the trite phrases of the Court of
Love could express this reality? The perfect romance of their
lives together would have no further lines.

But while the priests chanted requiems and incense rose to
God, would it not be possible to make one last tribute to
his lady? What about the poets who were always turning
out lyrics to celebrate the charms of this or that fair creature?
What of Geoffrey Chaucer, whom the Duke had noticed
at Hatfield a dozen years before and had seen off and on ever
since, a fellow who could turn a ribald jest, who had shrewd
comments to make at the expense of many a fool, who could
write extraordinary verse and yet could be trusted to be sensible? He was now Esquire of the King's household, and well
respected as such; in the present year he had fought in France.
Moreover he was doing a translation of the *Roman de la Rose*,
and had read some of it aloud. He could be relied on to
know tact and to command his speech. Let him be the means
of expressing our grief. A marginal note in a manuscript tells
that Chaucer was commissioned in some such way as this.

But marginal notes cannot always be trusted. Perhaps
there was a different scene. In such a loss, with the tragedy
of the Plague all round us, and the loveliness of the Duchess

in everyone's mind, no songs may be sung. It is a time for
cursing the ruler of the universe, who permits these outrages
to nature and to art. Or since bluster will not help, we may
sit in despair, while black garments keep the crowd away.
And yet, one man may approach. He is a good fellow, who
has amused us in better times with good humor and racy
anecdote, with a tact that never breaks the line between com-
moner and royalty, with soldier's manliness and poet's delicacy. His is a pious and sweet soul. He now has nothing to
say, but he falls on his knee and offers a manuscript which
contains a poem. In the verses written here there is nothing
mawkish, and so its sympathy can gain entrance and loose
the bonds of despair.

But what about Chaucer's difficulty in this task? Either
way there could be no false step; whether written by command or as a free offering of devotion, the poem had to be
at once intimate and humbly detached. A mere retainer could
not address the great Duke otherwise. Affection there might
be, implicit in the lines, but never too openly expressed. Affection even for the Duchess herself might be conveyed, but
the poet could not freely come out with it. How could any
dreamer, according to the conventions of the Court of Love,
dare to lift his eyes to Blanche, especially at such a time?
Chaucer set to work not without a consideration of pre-
cedent. There were no elegies he would care to copy. I do
not know whether he saw the *Regret de Guillaume*, written
as a lament for the death of the Duke's grandfather. But in
any case it was natural to turn to the literature of the Court
of Love, wherein poets had sung the praises of this lady and
that. The abler poets in France were still using the form,

and the convention had its freshness. To express grief in this
way would give every line a special meaning, just slightly
and not unbecomingly satirical or sophisticated, in a way appropriate for the court and yet not cynical. The poem must
keep every known feature of the literature of that type and
must echo as many examples of it as possible. There would
be the dream of the realm of love, or something of the sort.
Let the dreamer be an onlooker, a poor dolt who could
never quite understand what was taking place but whose
questions would reveal everything. Then the scene could
form itself after the pattern of Machaut's *Jugement dou Roy
de Behaingne*, where the knight debates whether it is better
to lose one's love by infidelity or by death. The dreamer
could elicit from the knight a full account of his great loss.
And no one could say whether the dreamer was the poet, or
whether the knight was precisely John of Gaunt.

So Chaucer may have approached the problem of composition, and proceeded to surround himself with works that
he could use or imitate. It is not the way writers do to-day.
But we know how Coleridge borrowed in a supremely
imaginative poem. With reference to his own stories Robert
Louis Stevenson confessed, "As if I had not borrowed the
ideas of half my own! As if any one who had written a story
ill had a right to complain of any other who should have
written it better!" Deschamps invited Chaucer to cull some
of the flowers in his literary garden, and the English poet
wasted no time but went ahead and did so. I wish I knew
how many of these passages he carried in his head, and how
many he took from the book as it lay on his table. No ordinary copybook could hold all the lines he took from other

writers and put to good use. A retentive memory he had no doubt; but I wonder whether that contained all the phrases from the *Roman de la Rose*, Boethius, Froissart, Machaut, Deschamps, and others, that he introduced by the way in his poetizing, together with the plots or schemes he imitated. Before books were printed, the epic memory held sway and did great service; and yet the precision of Chaucer's quotation makes me suspect that he also consulted the text.

In the *Book of the Duchess*, if he began with Machaut's poem, he seems to have been reminded at once of another by the same author, the *Dit de la Fonteinne Amoureuse*. Here the narrator has intimate converse with a prince, the dream motif is used, and the story of Ceyx and Alcyone is told furnishing the perfect counterpart for Chaucer's plot. An artless dreamer appears in Froissart's *Paradys d'Amour*; and Chaucer would be reminded of that because Froissart had used Machaut's poem. Thus the framework of the story became clearer; and ornamentation was added from the *Roman de la Rose*, details for the account of Fortune came from the *Remede de Fortune*, and, as we often hear, nearly every point in the description of the Duchess was taken from one or another French poem. With such evidence as this it is hard to imagine that any really literate person of the English court could miss the frequent verbal echoes of which the poem is composed. Anyone in the Duke's household who knew even a little foreign verse would, I believe, get the impression that here was a compost rich with plums from abroad, like the many poems which told of dream and dreamer, garden and lover, in the fair fields across the channel.

But the presiding deity here is Fortune rather than Venus. It is a striking fact. The fickle goddess, it is true, is known in other poems of the Court of Love and sometimes she is dominant; but here she alone rules. The meaning can only be that the deity who controls a world where things like Blanche's death can happen must indeed be capricious, ruthless, guided by no rational plan. Moreover there is another difference in this extraordinary elegy, from the ordinary run of Courtly Love poems, and that is something that also serves decidedly to mark it off from elegies in general. I refer to the element of humor. In the personifications, the apt speeches, the turns of plot, of the allegories of love, there is often wit but there is also humor. Perhaps it is intrinsic in the very nature of these poems, in the style of approach thus afforded to the lady, and in the mannerisms and gestures which it is the habit of this kind of verse to adopt. This is not strange. A dancing master always takes due precaution to teach his pupils to smile as they dance. The quality, something just a little more than a pleasant awareness of well being, is part of the grace of this type of expression. This, in any case, Chaucer slightly transforms and intensifies, perhaps because in the first instance he found it in his sources.

One may take almost any example. The *Roman de la Rose*, pattern for so many others, shows humor in its adventure of love, in terms of the garden and the rose. The same element appears in its pictures of Hatred, Felony, Villainy, Covetousness, and the rest, which Sir Mirth caused to be depicted on the garden wall, and again in the very conception of the porter Idleness and that of Love accompanied by "Douz Regarz," who has the two bows — one beautiful and comely, one ugly and gnarled, symbolizing a paradox that Chaucer remembered in his two inscriptions on the gate ˙n the *Parliament of Fowls*. The ingenuity of the plot itself shows the same spirit. For comparison one may turn to scenes in Spenser's poetry, where the beauty is richer and the humor attenuated. In the *Jugement dou Roy de Behaingne* of Guillaume de Machaut one finds it in the idea of the argument between the lady and the knight. One may indeed insist that this quality is what rescues the poetry of Courtly Love from insipidity. Chaucer was not likely to miss this aspect of its verse, and he had to retain it, not only to avoid monotony, but to remain loyal to the conventions of this *genre*. Yet he ran the risk of seeming flippant in an elegy; a literary conceit is more audacious than an ordinary metaphor and must wear its own excuse as obviously as one wears a chip on the shoulder.

But the fact is that the *Book of the Duchess* is all the more poignant because its pathos is not unrelieved. The idea of the bribe of the feather-bed for the God of Sleep, that too of the Cave of Sleep where the throng competes in sleeping, that of the puppy that guides the dreamer, many other details until the punning allusion to the Duke and Duchess at the end, show something very like levity or even the comic spirit. Against it there is, of course, the pathetic story of Ceyx and Alcyone; and in the second part the note of sadness, beginning with the loveliness of the May morning, the hunting of the deer that may not be captured, and the discovery of the knight singing his lay, is sustained. But the inconsequential development of the plot, noted by critics as essential to the dreamlike atmosphere, intensifying that idea as taken from other poems of the type, serves here an added purpose. It gives an air of irresponsible charm, and is no less than quietly amusing. In harmony with this appears the assumed stupidity of the dreamer, his unwillingness to understand what is going on, and, in the downpour of sorrow, his obstinate inability to come in when it rains. I emphasize the feature because it seems to be appreciated less than the same element in the *House of Fame* and the *Parliament*.

The young poet then showed special skill in avoiding the tedium which this style of poetry threatened to impose on his verse. Moreover he was enabled, by the dreamer's stupid questions, to insert a portrait of the Duchess and a complimentary description of her character. And there is an alchemy (that anticipates later transmutations of the kind in his verse) in his treatment of the emotional nature of his material so that grief is expressed but carries no burden with it. An elegy may cloy as much as too many flowers. But here Chaucer gently shakes his friend to bring him back to a sense of proportion. He acknowledges the full gravity of the loss, but he reminds us of the fundamental equilibrium in nature. The more inarticulate this dreamer becomes, the more the poem speaks. By his brief questions much is revealed; his fine understanding is shown by his dullness. His words at the last are packed:

> "Is that youre los? Be God, hyt ys routhe!"
> 1310.

With this exclamation comes the whole release: the huntsmen depart, the king goes home, we have Ceyx and Alcyone once more before us with the moral that it is vain to mourn.

"Now," says the poet, "I'll try to make a poem out of this dream." And the literal-minded will protest, "But he has!"

How did John of Gaunt feel as he read these lines for the first time? They are methodically narrative and yet somehow lyrical, dull with grief and yet happy. He must have had the excitement of discovering that the genius of the poet was here declared; and it is declared without pretentiousness, without fanfare or shaking of poetic locks. The essential rightness of the poet is visible in the whole plan of the poem. It implies, moreover, in the intricacy of its merits, that its reader would appreciate its values. Here was the bittersweet that might be missed by any but one perhaps who believed in the immortality of the soul, and that only a healthy genius could have conceived. No argument for immortality appears in the poem, it is true — not even in the story of Alcyone and her loss. On such a point, however, there is no reason to believe that the Duke, any more than the poet, had doubts. It is on the whole a matter of taste that Chaucer does not mention the doctrine, or essay at this time to talk religion with the bereaved John of Gaunt. But he does remind him of important things by the temper of his poem. Thus may the eminently sane speak in sorrow. The lugubrious tale of the knight in black and his lament — only a story so utterly trivial — could convey the full depth of the poet's comprehension. Might one take liberties with a duke in the fourteenth century when the sky was overcast and all England was in mourning? Only in terms of genuine affection, and that is what humor in this elegy means. The poet had been reading of queens' lives and of kings' and "many other little things," and then he dreamed of a knight who had lost his lady. "This was my dream. Now it is done."

That is not the tone of *Lycidas*, *Adonais*, or *Thyrsis*, where we are invited merely to weep or at least to recollect our emotion in tranquillity. One reason for the difference is that Chaucer's poem is touched with the high frivolity of Courtly Love; another is that obviously the writer's intention was to afford comfort to John of Gaunt. How far the poet was really intimate with the Duke has been a matter for much debate. From the theory that the relationship amounted to practically nothing at all, opinion has fluctuated to the suggestion that the Duke was a lover of Philippa and that Thomas Chaucer was his natural son. What is set down as scholarship must at times sound like gossip. All we know is that Chaucer wrote at least the *Book of the Duchess* in his behalf, and in 1374 got an annuity of ten pounds perhaps as belated thanks. The annuity seems too substantial and too much belated, however, for recognition of that kind. Chaucer's sister-in-law, Katharine Swynford, was John of Gaunt's household governess and mistress and eventually his third wife. The poet wrote (in what became the *Monk's Tale*) about Pedro of Castile, father of that Constance who was the Duke's second wife, and who, I think, receives a kind of indirect complimentary allusion in the saintly heroine of the *Man of Law's Tale*. Whether Lancaster had a taste for literature it is hard to discover, I suppose; but I sometimes wonder whether the knowledge in Spain of Gower's *Confessio Amantis* (dedicated to the Earl of Derby) did not follow Katharine's marriage to Enrique of Castile. In any case all the evidence of the *Book of the Duchess* points to the idea that the poet counted on a sensitive understanding in his reader, and on a friendliness that reached across barriers.

2

The result of a poetic success, like that of scandal, is that it must go on. The poet must write again and again and for every occasion that gives him warrant. In the achievement represented by the elegy there is full promise, I think, that he will be asked to write other occasional poems, and what is more, that the Lancaster family would be the most likely, among the first perhaps, to request performances of this kind. The family was, as people say, "literary": we can tell that from the Earl of Derby's negotiations with Gower, and his subsequent patronage, as Henry the Fourth, of Gower and Hoccleve; it is suggested in Deschamps's complimentary poem to Philippa of Lancaster, and in Hoccleve's similar tribute to Joan Beaufort. I can work out a very neat interpretation of the *House of Fame* and the *Parliament of Fowls* with reference to the family, and indeed someone else has done as much for the second of these poems. We may observe that the eagle was used as a symbol by John of Gaunt; Gower makes reference to it, and his French *Balades*, which seem to echo the *House of Fame*, the *Parliament*, and even the *Book of the Duchess*, were dedicated to Henry the Fourth. Perhaps the ruby in the ring (or that in the brooch) of Chaucer's *Troilus* is the same as that referred to in John of Gaunt's will, as "mon meillour cerf ov le bonne rubie," which he left to Katharine Swynford. (The word "cerf" may mean *jewel*.) To expound such theses, however, I am hesitant until Professor Manly discovers something in some letter, perhaps, to demonstrate the meaning of the allusions so that we may shake Chaucer's eagles by the bills, as the poet expresses it, so palpable will they be. Yet that the *House of Fame* and the *Parliament* contain personal references I feel certain, and whatever they conveyed to whoever properly understood them, the message was not stern.

They also show in part what the poet was doing with his time. After the business of the day was over he got off by himself and covered what most men would have thought was a vast amount of reading. He kept up with the literary vogue, the literature of Courtly Love. He picked up his Ovid from time to time; his copy of the *Metamorphoses* was well thumbed. Virgil he knew and respected. In both cases, however, he found it convenient to have a French rendering near by, the *Ovide Moralisé* and the *Roman d'Enéas*, which were classical with a difference. When he wanted to consult a Latin document, it appears, he got some help from a French or — in the case of the *Heroides* — even an Italian version. Thus he satisfied his scholar's zeal for information and kept the amateur's freedom from pedantry; he also missed something of the classical spirit. He read a great amount of allegory, and at first, I think, his favorite reading apart from Ovid was the *Roman de la Rose*. It is possible and even likely that in the same period he became acquainted with those romances he made fun of in later life, *Horn Child*, *Bevis of Hampton*, *Guy of Warwick*, *Libeaus Desconnus*, and the like. Possibly we should add stories of Isolde, Lancelot, Guinivere. But at its best this romantic literature did not stamp its character upon his early writing, which is marked rather with the elegant patterns of the love-vision.

Imagine then what it was like for Geoffrey Chaucer to go to Italy! English culture, despite the shocking contrasts of the Middle Ages, has always been a little like its scenery. It is never less than discreet, and the virtue of the Englishman is a matter of never forgetting how a gentleman may act. Puritanism — and by the word I do not refer simply to morality — is really of British stock, the spinster sister of the English squire. Continental puritans are isolated like Calvin, or as with St Augustine the tendency is acquired. When a young Englishman of the fourteenth century, sensitive to color and alive to emotion, went to Italy and saw for the first time the paintings, the architecture, and the general pre-occupations of a land warm with beauty, he must have been struck with amazement. Did Chaucer witness the gorgeous-ness of the wedding of Lionel Duke of Clarence and Violante in 1368 in Milan? If it took him but thirty days to come home again and use the passport prepared for him for another journey, perhaps he did. At any rate he got to Italy by 1372. There Barnabò of Visconti was in good form. I do not know how early the poet came in contact with that lurid figure with his background of sumptuous banquet, drunken brawl, lechery and murder; but he had dealings with the man in 1378. Great Barnabò of Visconti, god of delight and scourge of Lombardy, "Why sholde I nat thyn infortune acounte?" And so later he did write of him along with other notables, Hercules, the King of Spain, Nebuchadnezzar, and the rest. But such a person must have made characters in the *Roman de la Rose* look like stained glass.

Petrarch, the laureate poet, and Boccaccio too were there, and one could even get their manuscripts. I wish I knew how much they cost, but I feel sure that for Chaucer they were extremely expensive and at the same time priceless. Here was prime entertainment. But what did it mean for him to read Dante's *Divine Comedy?* Nothing in French allegory, or the verse of Guillaume de Guileville, or in moral treatises, or in the *Vision of Piers Plowman*, showed such depths. Here was an intelligence that Chaucer could understand, but one that surpassed his own. Jean de Meun was trivial beside such a writer, Ovid superficial, St Bernard narrow. Going through the folios of the *Commedia* must have been an artistic experience exciting beyond all others for the poet, but one, I suspect, of which the Englishman in him was fearful. Yet Chaucer could not resist the poem. He translated the story of Ugolino, one of the most horrible passages in the *Inferno*; he learned by heart and used the prayer to the Virgin in the ecstatic language of St Bernard in the *Paradiso*. This suggests the range of his response. I wish I could see him as he turned over these leaves in his room in England, and followed Dante's lead as Dante followed Virgil, down into Hell and up the mountain of Purgatory and then, with Beatrice as guide, took his flight through the spheres to the beatific vision. A literary excursion like this Chaucer could never talk about to others, but the impression was upon him.

Yet he was a busy man, and the Custom House, one may suppose, left him little time for contemplation. He was temperamentally a spectator of the social life of his day. There is abundant evidence that he was a good mixer and liked people. Gossip in high places informed him of an important betrothal, among friends really, and at his very doors — which may mean near Aldgate or simply in London. He had to send his own expression of pleasure in these tidings, but not too freely. Who is he after all to give poetic sanction to an affair concerning royalty? Rumor had given him the information, let Rumor reveal it. And this deity in Virgil is called Fama. But she was not so familiar a deity as certain others in allegory, and so the poet found out what he could about her where he could. Perhaps he consulted the learned and important manual *De Genealogia Deorum*, written by Boccaccio, and available in its first form by 1378. If he heard of it in Italy, I feel confident that Geoffrey Chaucer would have tried to find a copy. It seems likely that Gower knew and used it. If Chaucer actually had access to this book, he would have read here a description of Fama as a lady of varying stature, very like an eagle with feathers furnished with eyes, who dwelt in the middle region between earth and heaven. In other words here he would have been directed by specific quotation to the passages in Virgil and Ovid which he utilized.

But the journey to her abode, how should it be taken? It might well be a long, instructive tour. Unconsciously perhaps his imagination still held certain impressions he had gained from Dante; if so they were supplemented by thoughts of the travels that one often finds in medieval romance and allegory. Alexander traveled by air, according to the romances, and Ovid told of the flight of Icarus. But since Fame's abode according to Ovid was on a mountain Chaucer would be reminded of the strange journey to Fortune's house on a rocky height in the *Anticlaudianus* of Alain de L'Isle, and that in turn would recall the flight with birds to Fortune's house on the rock of ice in the *Panthère d'Amours* of Nicole de

Margival. With what bird should Chaucer travel, what better than the eagle whose symbolism was borrowed for Fame?
At one time Dante dreamed, he said, that the bird of Jove
carried him to the skies in that way. So the elements for the
poem are gathered, and the customary vision of Courtly
Love is suggested again, but again much modified. In general
following the *Panthère*, with a slight change in the sequence
of episodes, Chaucer planned first the visit to the temple of
Love, where he could present the story of Aeneas, to whom
many a royal line was traced in medieval narrative, and
where he could set forth the warning against faithlessness in
love, apparently essential to his purpose. The dreamer in
Nicole de Margival's poem visited Venus and then found
himself in a desolate region, from which the story leads on
to the scene of Fortune's lofty abode. So Chaucer, who
knew the motif of the desert of love in the poetry of Courtly
Love, and who always represents himself as unsuccessful in
affairs of the heart, could show himself lost in such an arid
waste. The desert in the *Panthère* recalled perhaps the parched
region in the *Inferno*, where flakes of fire tormented the suf-
ferers, and where Dante shortly takes off on the back of the
monster Geryon to fly to still lower depths of horror. Thus
Chaucer, moving about where no love is, could be rescued
by the eagle and borne aloft on a personally conducted tour
to realms above, with a lecture on the way to explain the
mechanism of the House of Fame and the rumor factory.
We need not deal with sources further.

The point is simply that the best science of the day could
be drawn upon to explain how gossip reaches Fame and
is again dispersed. Thus realism can again supplement ro-

mance; the flight with the eagle would not be so delightful
if the artificial manner of most allegories had been here retained. The realism of the rumor factory — when the poet
enters the turning walls, they seem to stop, as they naturally
would seem to in actual experience — is masterly despite
the extravagant and even fantastic details.

In some such way as this the *House of Fame* came into being. Its purpose, I think, is obviously to deal with some of
the fruits of gossip and its theme is love. Tidings of love
which the poet received were what he was about to dissemi-
nate when he composed this intricate narrative. A faithful
realist might protest nowadays that we need nothing so
complicated to set forth Chaucer's interest and delight in
the gossip, whatever it was. True enough, and so the cloudy
towers of Fame's palace and the turning factory of rumors
have the quality of humor. But again it is a tactful humor.
These images are at once wholly confined to the imagination
and yet entirely real. Apparently there is nothing personal
in the satire, and at times the poet seems to be in earnest
about his subject matter. Just when the man of great authority comes on the scene and the crowd scrambles up to
hear him, we are ready for something true in the way of
news, but — the manuscript breaks off. Was the completed
poem left in the heritage of the family of John of Gaunt or
the royal household? Shall we ever know? But here is humor
combined with fancy in a delicate pattern of adventure, and
dedicated, I believe, to the celebration of a distinguished
betrothal, one perhaps on everyone's lips but not quite
sealed in actuality.

Moderns sometimes do not care for the poem. After the

sixteenth-century voyages to the new world, and the later
excursions in the telescope and even with the balloon up to
the heavens, the old journeys to mythic realms ceased to
fascinate. As for the humor, we are told that what we have
here is chiefly humor of situation. Certainly that is revealed
in the poet's helplessness in the desert of love, and even in
Geoffrey's discomfort in his flight with the eagle. In metrical
form, in tone, in procedure, the poem is written in great
good spirits. Mistaken as the judgment was which found in
it a parody of the *Divine Comedy*, one can see in this idea a
happy fallacy as far as the indication of mood is concerned.
What medieval journey to romantic or symbolic realms was
ever touched with fun in this way? We can tell from the
spirit of the author that the tidings, whatever they are, will
be good. Yet the poem offers humor of character too, as
readers have a few times observed with regard to the eagle,
and as they might have added with reference to the types
demanding fame. Fame herself is living. It is, of course, a part
of her business to be arbitrary, and so almost automatically
she has that paradoxical element which gives a third dimension even to symbolic figures. But in her emotion, as in her
rage at the seventh company, who want an undeserved
reputation, there is the breath of life. All through the scene
there is the humor of at least traits of character. As for the
eagle, here the poet anticipates his best, in the bird's pride
of learning (he can lecture "lewedly to a lewed man"), in his
academic jokes uttered with the right academic manner, and
in his solicitude for his pupil. The poet has sacrificed his own
gravity to the picture; he has let himself be carried away by the
idea. Most significantly of all, he obviously likes the eagle.

Humor is of the very stuff of the poem. It is found in its conception, in the dignified sources chosen for the long disquisition, even in the details of the symbolism. The lapidaries, Boethius, the *Somnium Scipionis*, and many another solemn authority, have been called upon to give substance to this rich adventure. From Dante come lines in the Proem to the Second Book and in the Invocation at the beginning of the Third that show forth queerly in their new context, as embodying almost a mock solemnity. One can feel the poet's own relish in the adaptation, as if we were to observe something of Chaucer's mood while he worked. He read Dante's lofty appeal to the Muses to assist him in describing the appalling journey through Hell — one of the most deeply affecting experiences in the whole realm of literature.

> O mente, che scrivesti ciò ch'io vidi
> Qui si parrà la tua nobilitate.
> *Inf.* ii, 8–9.

Then, with reference to his blithe excursion to the windy halls of Fame, Chaucer almost flippantly says:

> O Thought, that wrot al that I mette,
> And in the tresorye hyt shette
> Of my brayn, now shal men se
> Yf any vertu in the be,
> To tellen al my drem aryght.
> 523–527.

We need not suppose that here he was smiling inwardly at Dante, or anything of the sort. But he must have felt pleasure in the incongruity of their setting when he took over these great lines. It is, in a way, the counterpart of what he did

when he borrowed the apparatus of the Court of Love for
his elegy. It is also what many poets of Courtly Love did
when they transferred the apparatus of the Church to their
very secular poems. In that case, however, the humor was
meant to be shared by the reader; here I wonder whether
any Englishmen knew Dante well enough to identify a passage like this. Rather I think we here see something of
Chaucer's enjoyment which he kept to himself. He did not
mark this indebtedness.

3

The same humor appears again in the composition of the
Parliament of Fowls. The first line shows it, where the general
aphorism of Hippocrates (taken from whatever intermedia-
ries) "ars longa, vita brevis" is applied strictly to the art of
love as if that had always been its meaning. Then the detailed paraphrase of the *Somnium Scipionis*, a treatise with
solemn intent if ever there was one, as an introduction to the
dream of a bird parliament on St Valentine's Day, strikes us
with wonder. The poet found a reference to it at the beginning of the *Roman de la Rose* as an example of the importance of dreams, and so he was prompted to use it. But why
did he have to follow Africanus in his exploration of the
spheres and his glance at this little earth and his moral regarding the danger of vice and the need of attention to the
"common profit," if all he intended to do was to put into
allegory something about the negotiations for some gentle
lady's hand?

> And he seyde, "Know thyself first immortal,
> And loke ay besyly thow werche and wysse

To commune profit, and thow shalt not mysse
To comen swiftly to that place deere
That ful of blysse is and of soules cleere.

"But brekers of the lawe, soth to seyne,
And likerous folk, after that they ben dede,
Shul whirle aboute th'erthe alwey in peyne,
Tyl many a world be passed. . . ."
                              Parliament, 73–81.

"Know thyself first immortal!" Thus speaks Africanus in ringing words. I cannot help suspecting a message here, underneath the rose of the symbolism, and possibly that of the Lancasters, of serious import half flippantly put for someone whose dignity can only be touched in this way. In the lofty view of life presented in this extensive paraphrase, Chaucer flew higher than ever he did in the *House of Fame*:

Thanne tolde he hym, in certeyn yeres space
That every sterre shulde come into his place
Ther it was first, and al shulde out of mynde
That in this world is don of al mankynde.
                              67–70.

A curious way to start, but not so strange if his point is briefly to admonish the young earl or prince for whom the poem is a compliment.

But far more amazing than all this is Chaucer's borrowing of lines from Dante's description of the gate of Hell to fit them, with all their horror still upon them, and expand them for the gate of the Garden of Love. How many of his readers in his own day could he expect to recognize what he had done? This transfer is more easily to be discovered than that already noted in the beginning of the Second Book of the *House of Fame*. But I doubt whether there were many besides possibly John Gower who could be counted on to see what had happened. In the case of the *Somnium Scipionis* he named his source and obviously expected his readers to know what was going on; but not so here. Once, presumably, he had himself been stirred by those sinister words which crowned the entrance to the dark and hopeless abyss in which all men of the fourteenth century still believed:

> "Per me si va nella città dolente;
> Per me si va nell' eterno dolore;
> Per me si va tra la perduta gente."
> *Inf.* iii, 1–3.

Then for the purposes of his allegory he wrote:

> "Thorgh me men gon into that blysful place
> Of hertes hele and dedly woundes cure"

and so on (*Parl.* 127 ff.). As Virgil took Dante's hand and led him into the dark plain, so Chaucer tells us that while he stood in doubt Africanus seized him and pushed him into the Garden of Love. What things happened in those gardens, and what associations they had! We remember the scene where Pandarus is leading Troilus to the room where Criseyde sleeps. "Artow agast so that she wol the bite?" he asks the timid youth.

What does it mean? Are we to suspect that fundamentally Chaucer had been unmoved by the lines in the *Inferno*? On artistic grounds alone the chance of such a lack of response is unlikely. He shows again and again that he has been deeply moved by Dante. As some scholars think, the lovely bit in

the present poem about the softness of the wind is a detached
echo of something in the *Purgatorio*:

> Therwith a wynd, unnethe it myghte be lesse,
> Made in the leves grene a noyse softe
> Acordaunt to the foules song alofte.
>
> 201–203.

The passage seems closely related to the following:

> Un' aura dolce, sanza mutamento
>   Avere in sè, mi feria per la fronte
>   Non di più colpo, che soave vento.
> Per cui le fronde, tremolando pronte,
>   Tutte quante piegavano a la parte
>   U' la prim' ombra gitta il santo monte —
> Non però dal lor esser dritto sparte
>   Tanto che li augelletti per le cime
>   Lasciasser d'operare ogni lor arte. . . .
>
> *Purg.* xxviii, 7–15.

Here the English poet seems to have remembered the description because it is so sensitively close to nature. He has
not gone back to the original to force a verbal approxima-
tion; he has simply remembered it and reproduced it with
a difference in itself felicitous. The borrowing reveals the
poet's taste. But we can hardly pause here for a list of the
numerous passages where the flotsam and jetsam of his imagination carried a favorite phrase or two from the *Divine
Comedy*. Was the subject-matter of the account of the gate
of Hell such as to leave him unstirred? Was he, in other
words, fundamentally cynical? His religious preoccupations,
of which I shall say more later, are enough to make that impossible. The idea of Hell as a single item of doctrine was

not one to worry men much in the fourteenth century. They were bound to accept it like any other.

In any case Chaucer seems to show a similar spirit with material from another and ultimately more sacred source. This is when he adapts lines from the *Roman de la Rose* which plainly echo the *Apocalypse*. He is telling of his Earthly Paradise of love:

> No man may there waxe sek ne old;
> Yit was there joye more a thousandfold
> Than man can telle; ne nevere wolde it nyghte,
> But ay cler day to any manes syghte.
>> *Parl.* 207–210.

Jean de Meun had written as follows:

> Jamais seif aveir ne pourront,
> E vivront tant come eus vourront
> Senz estre malades ne mortes.
>> *Roman de la Rose*, 20395–20397.

> Cist la nuit en essil enveie,
> Cist fait le jour que dit avaie,
> Qui dure pardurablement,
> Senz fin e senz comencement. . . .
>> *Ibid.*, 20559–20562.

Chaucer could hardly forget "And there shall be no more death, neither sorrow nor crying, neither shall there be any more pain . . ." ". . . For there shall be no night there." "And there shall be no night there; and they need no candle, neither light of the sun; for the Lord God giveth them light; and they shall reign for ever and ever." (*Rev.* xxi, 4 and 25; xxii, 5.) I cannot present here a close analysis of his indebtedness in the details of this remarkable garden, but I am in-

clined to think he went back to the *Apocalypse* at least for
the accent of his lines.

Chaucer's procedure here is like what he did in the *Merchant's Tale* in his use of material from the *Song of Songs*.
Here the Merchant greets his young wife in the morning
with lines that in substance for Christians had long meant
the call of Christ to His bride the Church:

> "Rys up, my wyf, my love, my lady free!
> The turtles voys is herd, my dowve sweete;
> The wynter is goon with alle his reynes weete."
> E. 2138–2140

The explanation in all these cases, I believe, is the same. The
attitude of the Middle Ages to things sacred is marked with
a familiarity that seems strange to the modern, at least to
the modern who can discern what is sacred or remembers
reverence. For the Middle Ages, passages in literature or
Scripture have one meaning in their context and possibly
another as part of a general literary heritage, from which
any writer of the time could take what he liked and use it.
Chaucer showed no lack of understanding, no covert cynicism, when he borrowed from Holy Writ or from Dante and
put his gains to another use. But he does show another side
of his character in these adaptations. He must have been less
than human, when he took over Dante's account of the gate
of Hell and transferred it to Love, if he missed the comic
element in the metamorphosis.

There is nothing original in noticing that he often took
passages from serious works to get a humorous effect. But
my present point is that in the *Parliament of Fowls* and else-

where we sometimes find that apparently Chaucer meant the joke for himself alone. We seem indeed to have the privilege of catching the poet's smile when he is unaware that we are looking. We have a sense of the joy and also the fun he had in his writing. We know more surely what he himself was like. It is, I grant, a fine point, this special matter of the humor of sources; and I do not want to press it too far. But giving us a glimpse as it does of the personal features of Chaucer himself, I cannot let it be misunderstood or relinquished. He had fun in composing the *House of Fame* and the *Parliament of Fowls*; and even in the *Book of the Duchess* his spirit was warm with the kindliness of humor. One is attracted by that kind of man. One knows that he was good company. One would like to have seen him off duty and to have enjoyed his wit and his healthy mind in fields other than just literary. The same cannot be said of all authors. Of Horace no doubt and John of Salisbury, of St Thomas More, perhaps Henry Fielding, and at times Samuel Johnson — it would be interesting to draw up a complete list. But many writers, and especially satirists, give the impression that they were at times difficult. With Chaucer what one critic has referred to as the "engaging rascality and infinite *bonhommie*" of his characters appears everywhere in his own work.

What was the *Parliament of Fowls* written to set forth? Was it merely a *tour de force* of wit with reference to St Valentine's Day? I confess that such an explanation seems inadequate to me. Nor in the light of the symbolism of the *Book of the Duchess* do I feel required, as an alternative, to see in it a closely knit personal allegory with identifiable references at every point. Some lady's hesitation may be represented here as a compliment to her in terms of the eagle; but I do not think the same point could be made after wedlock. Allusions to the English parliament I believe there are. There is humor in casting the main characters as birds. Although one of the contestants makes a boast of long service, quite possibly the royal or noble figures behind the screen of symbolism were very young. That the formel eagle must have a year to decide may reflect a picturing of childhood attachments years before wedlock. We really know nothing about the meaning of the poem when it comes to the history it actually embodies. But that the bird parliament was chosen for this setting, and that all the birds gathered on this day to choose their mates with Nature as presiding officer, such a scheme has more than poetic value. Like the *House of Fame* this poem shows humor in its very conception. It may even be taken, since it deals specifically with the Court of Love, as flippant. The plot of the contending lovers, if such a motif exists, or the *demande d'amour*, is used for the special purpose of showing that in this case the rose may not be picked for yet many a day. Betrothals were attempted young in the Middle Ages. But whether we have here the story of Philippa of Lancaster or Katharine or even Elizabeth, or perhaps even the Earl of Derby (he was married about 1380), I doubt whether we shall ever know. I believe, however, that the match is projected rather than concluded, that indeed the poem represents the use of hints and suggestions to urge the lady. Here again it is not Venus who rules; in this case it is Nature. And she does not compel the formel eagle beyond endurance to make up her mind.

These poems based on the Vision of Courtly Love all show

marked differences from others of the type. Fortune rules in one; in another Fame: in the third Nature. It is true that we visit the temple of Venus early in the *House of Fame*, and we read much about her shrine; but the vital figure in the poem who controls all action is Fame herself. In the same way in the *Parliament* it is really Nature who is the dominant character. If my guess is justified, these poems all celebrate, from one angle or another, wedded-love. The vision they show does not, as in other poems of the type, tell us that Venus is favorably inclined so that the dreamer may have his *amie*. Nor does it appear that Chaucer spent much time in speculating on the allegorical appearance and conduct of fair "Cipride." In general the characters are like real people — the knight in black, the goddess Fame, the birds in the *Parliament* and the eagle in the *House of Fame*. Here we do not find elaborate displays of the plots and counterplots of Daunger, Paour, Honte, Doutance, Beauté, Honneur, Courtoisie, and the other abstractions that play about in so many allegories. When as in the *Parliament* we do get something of the sort — Plesaunce, Aray, Lust, and the other figures in the Garden of Love, with Dame Pees and Priapus and even Venus herself — it is brief and decorative, not a *psychomachia* but a tapestry as a background for the real story.

Realism affects the *dramatis personae*, the dialogue, the discourse of the eagle, the talk between the turtle and the duck, and even the technique of the dream. It sends just a breath, as we have seen, into the daintily planned garden of the *Parliament*, which otherwise belongs to the work of pigment or embroidery. There is, it is true, realism in certain other poems of the Court of Love, notably the *Roman de la Rose*, but not so pervasively. And with Chaucer one may notice that his genius did not take spontaneously and easily to an art of abstraction. It is evident as early as this that he cares more for people themselves than he does for generalizations about people. Given free rein he would probably never have used allegory at all; that he did adopt this method came from the fact that it was fashionable. It was the literary form to which a young man must adjust himself if he wished to be heard. But this young writer had no abstract view of life, and so he introduced material from life as he found it whenever he could. In each instance, the whole scheme of his poem is also informed with humor, which seems to prompt even the most fantastic details. Take, just for one trivial example, the lovely bit about the ladies with flowing hair who danced for ever about the temple of Love in the *Parliament*. Most of this material Chaucer got from Boccaccio, but he added one significant detail. The *Teseide* says merely the ladies were

> Discinte, scalze, in capelli e in gonne,
> E in ciò sol dispendevano il giorno.
> *Tes.* vii, st. 57.

But Chaucer adds that this was their perpetual duty: "That was here offyce alwey, yer by yeere." (*Parl.* 236.) His word "office" indeed suggests something religious, and one thinks of the Vestal Virgins. The ceremonial dance of these lovely creatures for ever continuing is delicious to contemplate. It is just the sort of final touch the poet usually adds to his borrowings, the lustre of perfection.

And yet in the structure of these poems, in their conception and accomplishment, how much is there that lays claim to the sublime? There is undoubtedly something of this when the poet utilizes the machinery of Courtly Love to convey with a saving element of humor his sympathy for the stricken John of Gaunt. I see it also in evanescent gleams in Nature's court held to settle the affairs of the eagles, in the garden beyond that gate whose inscription holds an everlasting ambiguity. There is something of it too in the marvelous flight with the eagle up to that rarefied atmosphere where stand the shifting towers of Fame. Indeed the moment when the poet, uplifted in the talons of his lecturer, objects to further learning, might suggest a specific example of this spacious achievement; but I am afraid that the episode lacks sufficient significance within the poem and universality without it to justify appreciation on that level. I wish we could read into the allegory some meaning such as that the poet has been surfeited with study and now at last seeks the real world and the gossip of friends; but that would be poor allegory as things now stand, and it does not work out that way. But the episode itself is superb and one to be grateful for. How different such flashes of humor are from the conceits and preciosity of other poems of the Court of Love, where the values are chiefly those of sentiment! Chaucer's early poems both gain and suffer from a lack of pretentiousness in this vein; it is perfectly obvious that he has no slightest thought of creating a great work of art with universal significance. Whatever flights he might attempt in that way, laughter would keep breaking through. He is too much in fun to have time for a strenuous attempt at being a genius. Realism and humor investing a sympathetic observation of human character, these qualities mark his early poems.

Chapter III

TROILUS AND CRISEYDE

THE MANUSCRIPTS that survive of Chaucer's *Troilus and Criseyde* tell us more about its composition than we know about that of any other poem he wrote. A study of the variant readings shows that it was revised at least once; that Chaucer added most of the long soliloquy on predestination in Book IV and extended the Epilogue. Other changes are incidental, but all of them make it certain that he took the greatest pains with this work, and that in writing the poem he was actuated by motives of fundamental earnestness. Among his longer productions, it is in many ways his most finished achievement. If in rich maturity of conception it may be rated somewhat below the "marriage cycle" of the *Canterbury Tales*, it nevertheless attains a fuller perfection within the limits of its own purpose. Its style is at once supple and marked with astonishing vitality; every theme it introduces — and there are many — it brings to an appropriate completion. The preoccupation of its story with the concerns of youth meant perhaps a lack of range in the artistic possibilities open to the poet's imagination, but the emotional patterns fell within correspondingly easier compass. Ironies of a youthful misadventure would seem to be more steadily congenial to Chaucer, or to the people for whom he was writing, than tragic implications of disaster among an older group. In any case the story suited his genius. It is a great poem.

If in the allegories Chaucer presented the Court of Love and its conventions somewhat humorously, he takes it seriously enough in the *Troilus*. This is no matter of wedded love; the affair is illicit enough to be kept secret, and all the mandates of love are exercised in full force. Mr. C. S. Lewis indeed has been rash enough to maintain that the poem was written in praise of this kind of thing. Chaucer himself calls it a tragedy. Presumably he might have chosen a plot where lovers who faithfully kept the rules of the game were brought to a happy ending, although as one recalls the stories of Tristram and Iseult, of Lancelot and Guinevere, of Paolo and Francesca, one may conclude that there were not many who came off on that high note of bliss. Perhaps the somber picture, the downward path, offers the more significant opportunity for a student of character. The plot, however, contains little that may be interpreted in favor of sporting with Amaryllis in the shade. On the contrary it presents a magnificent situation in terms of human weakness; and on those terms for artistic reasons alone Chaucer might have found abundant impulse for his imagination. He could heighten its qualities: enrich the lugubrious youthfulness of the lover; make Pandarus a little older to afford a better contrast to Troilus and to prevent his own failures in love from making him seem merely fatuous; and finally he could add to the complexity of his heroine's character, making her for one thing less accessible to her lover. But if the meaning of the story were utterly repugnant to him, would he have chosen it in the interests of art?

Theoretically, I suppose, a radical may write a play that preaches conservatism because it involves a fascinating problem in technique; but I do not find that this often happens. An indifferent radical might do so perhaps, but radicals are seldom indifferent. Nor do I find conservatives setting forth revolutionary literature. In any case the story of the *Troilus* as we first come upon it in the *Roman de Troie* and again as it appears in the *Filostrato* hardly suggests the permanent values of love. Chaucer altered it to the effect of deepening the sorrows of the lover and intensifying the infidelity of the lady and ending the poem with an interpretation which should leave no doubt as to the way Courtly Love appears when last we look upon it. As it stands, (the *Troilus* indubitably means that the affairs of Venus belong to human frailty,) and this conclusion agrees with what he elsewhere has to say on the subject. The *Legend of Good Women* emphasizes the fickleness of men and the sufferings of their ladies quite as often as it celebrates the heroism of Cupid's saints. In the "marriage cycle" of the *Canterbury Tales*, the love that seems most admirable is surely that of the wedded Griselda and Dorigen.

"Morality, heavenly link!" as the *Bab Ballads* have it — how we all to-day shy away from that theme! For us it is associated with inflexible moral codes and unpleasant moralists. It hardly seems possible nowadays that (with saints at least) morals once seemed positive, living, and even radiant. In medieval literature it was impossible to evade considerations of this kind, and didacticism penetrated not only allegory but romance as well. Chaucer in the *Troilus* shows that he is fully aware that he cannot neglect this aspect of his story. The Epilogue of the poem was added to interpret the plot against a Christian background. Starting with hints in Boccaccio the poet appealed to youth to turn from worldly love to love celestial, and he added the prayer to the triune God. Later he inserted the stanzas from Boccaccio's *Teseide* describing the flight of Arcite's soul, transferring them, of course, to Troilus, in order to give the young man the sort of bird's-eye view of life that, we remember, he himself had had in the *House of Fame*. It must be salutary to view life from the hereafter; it is certainly most helpful to look at love from a safe distance. And from the detachment of the eighth sphere, Troilus sees his own love affair and his tragedy as mere items in the news of the universe, as details in the history of human folly. The affairs of the Court of Love end this way after all. There are far greater concerns. The laugh of Troilus, as he looks back on all this, may not be ironical or bitter, but it is a laugh. And it is almost the first time Chaucer has told us of anything of the kind from his young hero.

I am afraid that modern critics do not like this laugh very much. It is a great pity. It came down through Boccaccio all the way from Lucan's *Pharsalia*; and Chaucer took the trouble to add it at this point where he must have been aware that it would have great importance. The last thing we hear from this young lover after all is not a sonnet, not a *planctus* to his lady, not a paean to those rapturous hours at the house of Pandarus, but a laugh. This is what is likely to stay in the memory. It is most disconcerting. But, first of all, let us be grateful for the fact that mirth at this moment in the poem robs it of sentimentality. If Chaucer adds a moral, he is not smug or complacent about it. And I believe the chief reason for a modern critic's dislike of this laugh is that he perceives it is also Chaucer's laugh, and that is another matter. We do not like to find the poet laughing at the tragedy, or the love affair, or especially that wonderful night of love at the house of Pandarus, a scene too exquisite to discount for moral considerations. It vexes the sense of beauty to be told that beauty was not all truth on that occasion. We would remind Geoffrey Chaucer that even he was stirred at the thought of the union of these irresistible lovers. Even he, the poet, rejoiced in the passion of his young hero, and perceptibly felt the soft delight of Cressid's lovely form. The poet's own thoughts were at least as daring as Troilus even after Pandarus bore away the candle to the chimney:

> Hire armes smale, hire streghte bak and softe,
> Hire sydes longe, flesshly, smothe, and white
> He gan to stroke . . .
>
> iii, 1247–1249.

Yes, but the poet's imagination was there first. These words go beyond anything we find in Boccaccio, and I feel certain that Chaucer exulted when Troilus took his lady in his arms and bade her yield.

But unfortunately that cannot be the only emotion he cherished in this scene. At the very time when the lovers are united, the poet knew what were going to be the fruits of this event. Could this blessed moment have been prolonged, then all were well. But these lovers are not married, they are living by the rules of the Court of Love, and furthermore they have the weaknesses of human nature. Even during

Criseyde's most passionate avowal of confidence and surrender, (Chaucer knew that she would betray her lover and
that before many moons she would be in the arms of another
man.) So against a greater background all this loveliness has
a quite different coloring. There is the coming of the day
upon this love-scene, heralded by Troilus's lines that make
us think of Romeo's supreme poetry at a corresponding
time:

> "O cruel day, accusour of the joie
> That nyght and love han stole and faste iwryen,
> Acorsed be thi comyng into Troye . . ."
> iii, 1450–1452.

"Look, love, what envious streaks . . .!" But Criseyde too
has expressed herself in similar vein about the "rakle nyght,"
and later she gives her devotion to Diomede, and despite her
reassuring words, perhaps to another after that. (And Troilus
is killed in battle, not in a superb combat — nothing grand
happened! — but just like any other man.) So after all one
may laugh as one looks back over the course of events even
to the blissful moments of the night so long sought for by
the twain. The laugh requires no bitterness or irony; only a
sense of proportion. Chaucer is never destructive.

It is not with him a question of kindliness breaking
through a sterner purpose; his philosophy is kindly. So here
he would say, I think, that (the love of Troilus is ultimately
frustrated, but it is definitely a good as far as it goes.) It is not
to be confused with the "blynde lust" (blind pleasure) which
he later condemns, to which Troilus and Cressid yield in
their longing for each other, and which has to do with the

self-indulgence of passion. When the hero and heroine make simply an episode of their love, then its significance is cheapened. But potentially, as Troilus himself so buoyantly sang, it is the same as the love that turns the sun and the other stars, it might have had a sacramental permanence, and we may well rejoice in its potentialities and its beauty.

The scene at the house of Pandarus has also another significance, I think. It shows that Chaucer had a normal interest and delight in human passion. There is so much in his later writing to suggest matrimonial bitterness, and in one way or another he so often suggests his own ill-success in love, that before long some critic will probably make psychological deductions not favorable to the poet's normal outlook upon life. There are several stories where he refers to a more or less bestial variety of satisfaction. Here at least he gives a picture of two lovers meeting in a union that (whatever be the fulness of their passion) in and for itself is wholly untainted, wholly beautiful, with an extraordinary lyric quality in its presentation, and a vitality that carries it with a splendid sweep. Of all this, however, I shall have more to say later. Now I may simply add that the perfection of this picture is not only of value for itself but contributes enormously to the tragedy when it comes — the lovelier, the more appealing, the scene where Troilus and Criseyde are united, the darker and more grievous the destruction of all this by infidelity.

I admit, I think quite freely, the beauty of this scene. And I believe trouble is caused in criticism because the modern is afraid that we must ignore the full value of all this if we grant moral considerations any validity at all. To protect us from that he is likely to form his interpretation of the poem on a radically different basis. He will reject the evidence of those stanzas where the poet has unmistakably declared a Christian philosophy. The result is an interpretation which is different from the poet's. The love scene in Book III, your critic will argue, is wholly admirable; that is the part that Chaucer really cared about. Whatever conflicts with that must have been added for some artistically unworthy motive, and so we find ourselves in the presence of an attack on the poet himself. This, however adroitly concealed or overlooked, is really of first importance. Chaucer, we may be told, was fundamentally not serious. Matthew Arnold said as much years ago for reasons of his own, and he is quoted approvingly by Sir Arthur Quiller-Couch, who nevertheless proceeds to admit that the closing stanzas of the *Troilus* have high seriousness. Another writer has urged that the poet was at heart a cynic, following conventional morality (with uncomfortable hypocrisy) in early life and breaking forth with his true nature in after years in that unrestrained revelry of composition which is the Wife of Bath. The dividing line comes at about the time of the *Troilus*. The Epilogue shows the poet's pretence of high and noble things; the frankly sensual poem reveals the real man underneath. For the moment I may simply remark that there is nothing in the portrayal of the Wife of Bath that implies a cynical attitude toward life in Chaucer himself, and, even if there were, the *Franklin's Tale* would serve to balance the view.

Closely related to the accusation that the poet was cynical, is the charge that he was unconcerned about moral issues, and revelled irresponsibly in the emotional ups and downs of his characters, regardless of what they all meant. Why not? the modern may ask, who regards anything else as superstition and irrelevance. But a critic of that type is himself a cynic and can see no important significance in art except as entertainment. For such a reader the Epilogue is a sop to the pious. *Troilus and Criseyde* is for him an experience rather than an idea. And then there is another theory that closes the door to criticism: Chaucer, we are told, was of his own age, and into his thinking we may scarcely penetrate, partly because that was restricted by various limitations now difficult to bear in mind or even to imagine as we attempt to reconstruct his views. A critic of this stamp will accept what he finds in fourteenth-century literature without attempting to explain or understand it. When a long discourse appears in a work, he will say that such a digression seems absurd now but men in those days wrote in a fashion that we can hardly hope to understand. Perhaps they liked to be sententious or edifying; at any rate it is a blemish and we will pass it by.

Obviously all these points involve matter of the greatest importance for our understanding of Chaucer's genius and also of his character. If he wrote only for entertainment, if the moral patterns of life did not enter his aesthetic scheme, if art to him is in no sense a matter of illumination or insight, then I would insist that his production belongs on a level below that of great genius. If he is fundamentally cynical, and if we mean by the term that he had no belief in the ultimate significance of anything, then I find his art spurious. He will shift from satire to sentimentality unconcerned as to how valid what he offers may be. For if he sees meaning in life, what is an experience must also be an idea. Ultimately he is bound to estimate the love affair of Troilus not only as a thing of beauty but as a cause with effects and an effect of causes. If we really cannot read Chaucer's intention in his works, then we can hardly criticize them adequately. To say that we are hopelessly prone to read into the poet's mind and into the thoughts of his characters the ideas of our own period is hardly worth the utterance; on its own terms it is insecure. For if Chaucer is a genius and his characters truly live, then they are proper stuff for the researches of the most modern criticism and psychology with direct reference to life. If the poet's wisdom and humor seem the richer in the light of a modern approach, then there is a strong chance that this method is getting at the truth. To be specific, where we deny that Chaucer could have regarded something as comic or ironic (since in his day men commonly took a solemn view of such things), we forget the perennial insight of humor — humor, that is, in a genius of serious purpose.

At first sight readers may be quite perplexed by the tone of the *Troilus*. The verses weep as he writes, says the poet. He is to tell the double sorrow of Troilus, how the young man went from woe to weal and from weal to woe in his love affair. Only the Fury Tisiphone may be invoked for such a tale. Well, it hardly sounds the really tragic motif, does it? The orchestra does not strike the deeper notes at all. A gloomy face befits a sorrowful narrative, yes, but isn't someone pulling it a bit long? The mood seems to be reflected even in what he says about that most sacred of subjects, love *paramours*:

> For I, that God of Loves servantz serve,
> Ne dar to Love, for myn unliklynesse,
> Preyen for speed, al sholde I therfore sterve,
> So fer am I from his help in derknesse . . .
>
> i, 15–18.

and so on. Need I say, he certainly did not expect to die? The bidding prayer that comes later, and all the apparatus of the Church of Love, even to Troilus's litany in distress to the gods, are in harmony with the peculiar humor of this type of machinery in Court of Love literature; but here in the present background in relation to the tone of the poem as a whole it seems peculiarly apt. An almost jocular note creeps in at times:

> The dayes honour, and the hevenes yë,
> The nightes foo — al this clepe I the sonne —
>
> ii, 904–905.

Such an expression is not out of place in the *Knight's Tale*, the *Merchant's Tale*, or the *Franklin's Tale*; but on the face of things, isn't it a little odd in a tragedy? Of course we know that Chaucer customarily has a pleasant manner, and likes to dig his reader in the ribs now and then, but certainly these verses do not weep. The puns too on the names of Troy and Calchas, how out of place one might consider them! The poet seems to be thoroughly enjoying himself, with a strange detachment, in narrating the sad course of events in this his "little tragedy." Was he really untouched by what happened? I have already confessed that I think he was moved, far more, I may now add, than in the *Knight's Tale*, where at times the mood is similar. The fact is that his poem is shot through, iridescent, with irony. It is not somber or grave; it is managed with a light touch. But it is irony none the less, and for a proper understanding of the lines we must see it when it appears.

Why then does he adopt this manner in the *Troilus*? The reason is, I think, that he is dealing with youth and with the affairs of youth, which are after all on a different level from that of great tragedy. Troilus shows, it is true, the classic flaw, ἀμαρτία, human frailty; but his is a rather general weakness as young men go. He has hardly more than the pride of youth and early passions. The logic of his case hardly calls for disintegration of character and final destruction. It is in harmony with this view and with the tone of the poem that neither he nor Diomede kills the other; that indeed nothing magnificent occurred. His laugh at the end is in the same key. Chaucer's manner has been described elsewhere as that of sympathetic irony, and the phrase is exact. From beginning to end in telling this story the speaker's voice suits the attitude which is expressed in the Epilogue: "Swich fyn hath, lo, this Troilus for love!" (v, 1828). His "grete worthynesse," "his estat real," and "his noblesse," they all come to the same end. The poet has sometime before expressed his regret, it is true, that Cressid bestowed Troilus's gift on Diomede, and comments that "that was litel nede"; he says he would excuse Cressid's falseness, if he could, just out of pity. But these things are incidental, and sink out of significance before the larger view we obtain at the end of the poem. In short the tragic mood of the poem is one which suits the age of the participants in the story, without, however, any trace of condescension.

In the light of such considerations can anyone doubt how we are to interpret the poem as a whole? Certain passages in the love-scene and others even earlier have been taken to afford a direct inconsistency with the Epilogue. Let us examine some of these:

> Forthy ensample taketh of this man,
> Ye wise, proude, and worthi folkes alle,
> To scornen Love, which that so soone kan
> The fredom of youre hertes to hym thralle;
> For evere it was, and evere it shal byfalle,
> That love is he that alle thing may bynde,
> For may no man fordon the lawe of kynde.
>
> i, 232–238.

This, of course, is merely an expression of the controlling power of passion — a fact that no one in the Middle Ages would deny, whether the ecclesiast or the scholastic philosopher. If you give yourself up to this passion, then, alas, the end may be like that of Troilus. The Epilogue neatly caps this very passage with specific allusion, it would almost seem, to the wise and proud and worthy. Such was the end, we are there told, of our hero's "grete worthynesse" and all the rest of it. But what of another passage in the poem that seems to furnish an even greater inconsistency? There we read:

> Thei callen love a woodnesse or folie,
> But it shall falle hem as I shal yow rede;
> They shal forgon the white and ek the rede,
> And lyve in wo, ther God yeve hem meschaunce,
> And every lovere in his trouthe avaunce!
>
> iii, 1382–1386.

This stands in even more violent contrast, one might infer, to the lines in the Epilogue where Chaucer altered a passage of the *Filostrato* to read as follows:

> O yonge, fresshe folkes, he or she,
> In which that love up groweth with youre age,
> Repeyreth hom fro worldly vanyte,
> And of youre herte up casteth the visage
> To thilke God that after his ymage
> Yow made, and thynketh al nys but a faire
> This world, that passeth soone as floures faire.
>
> v, 1835–1841.

But are we to suppose that, when Chaucer made his careful revision of the poem, he let a glaring inconsistency stand? If we had to choose, could we doubt which passage represents the deeper, the considered view of the situation? Or shall we suppose that the poet's nature is divided between the two attitudes here revealed so that fundamentally he could not decide which was the nearer to the truth? Of course in the general tone of the poem it is plain that the first passage is lightly ironic and the second is directly sincere. We do not really have to question both the poet's personal integration and his artistic honesty if we recognize the fact that Chaucer deals with Troilus's love in somewhat the same way as he deals with the young man himself. Let no one suppose that either is unimportant! Beware of taking this matter of love too flippantly: behold what it has done to our young hero, who mourns the livelong day and at night sleeps no more than does the nightingale! Nay, he wallows and weeps like Niobe the Queen!

The poem is perfectly unified on these terms. It is not fair to cite as a parallel such works as the sonnets of Petrarch, where at one time the poet expresses devotion to Laura, at another accuses her of separating him from God. Such sentiments are of the extravagances of love, and sonnets in any case hardly require the unity of a story. The fact is, the whole structure of the *Troilus* shows that Chaucer left nothing to chance or inconsistency in its arrangement. He was far too much in earnest about its composition, which in the proems, the interweaving of borrowings, the use of Boethius, the development of the characters, the lyrics introduced, shows the most painstaking attention to detail. Thoughtful readers have noted the intricacy of its pattern. Not adequately observed, however, has been the symmetry, the balance, of its episodes and use of material. I may therefore mention a few examples to show how conscious the poet was, at every moment, of the problem of disposing his material effectively and to the point. Hector, touched by Criseyde's beauty, urges her to stay in Troy; and, when her father makes the move later to get her exchanged for Antenor, it is Hector again who works in her behalf to keep her in the city. Pandarus comes in when Troilus bewails his new and hopeless love; it is Pandarus again in Book IV who comes in to find the hero in despair at Criseyde's leaving. Troilus sings of his love in Book I, and again in despair in Book V; the lovers exchange letters at the beginning of their affair, and again after their separation; the ladies are reading of Thebes in Book II, and Cassandra expounds the story in Book V; Criseyde dreams of her newly found love, and later Troilus dreams of his lady's infidelity; it may even not be fanciful to see in Diomede's offer to be Criseyde's brother a parallel to Criseyde's earlier offer to be a sister to Troilus. And finally, as a student suggests to me, Troilus begins by smiling at love and lovers, and ends in the skies laughing at about the same thing. These and other instances, and even parallels within the episodes, offer an important means of achieving dramatic irony. It is easy to compare the original vows of hero and heroine with what they actually do later. One may contrast the love-scene itself, and its attendant comment on people who dispraise love, with the story as a whole and the comment in the Epilogue. This type of inconsistency is, as many examples in literature show, of the very essence of irony. Thus the dreams of the glory of kingship and power shared by Lord and Lady Macbeth stand in contradiction to their ultimate suspicions, murder, and frustration. So too the joyful devotion of Othello and Desdemona finds contradiction in the jealousy that snuffs it out. When Tristram and Iseult drink the love-potion and gaze into each others eyes, the scene has lasting beauty but derives color from the subsequent tragedy. A fundamental inconsistency in the *Troilus* would be an amazing breach in a poem where every part has been planned so closely with reference to every other part.

There is symmetry in the framework of the poem as a whole. Troilus sins against the Court of Love by his youthful arrogance and he suffers for it; in the Christian setting he sins in his dalliance with love *paramours* and he suffers for it. Criseyde sins against the Court of Love by infidelity and suffers for it; in the Christian setting as well she sins like Troilus, only far more grievously, and she makes a greater retribution. Criseyde's sin of infidelity is greater from both points of view than any other, and the deeper effect on her character is obvious. "To Diomede algate I wol be trewe") shows that this lovely creature, who had taken pride in always facing the facts, now longs desperately to deceive herself. It is a sinister warning of things that may yet occur. Incidentally we may observe that the sins include those that mark great tragedies, pride and disloyalty. And when I study the characters in more detail, I hope to show that Pandarus too shares in the moral scheme I have just indicated. There may be some question, on the other hand, whether dalliance with love may properly be included among the sins according to the medieval way of dealing with such things. In fact certain modern studies have found the Middle Ages rather confused on the subject, divided between a pagan and a Christian view, with the Christian view itself far from clear. Since this is precisely the charge that has been brought against Chaucer and the *Troilus* I may be pardoned for dwelling on it for a moment.

There were of course the remains of a pagan tradition of love in medieval writings. According to this view the worship of Venus and Cupid was a diversion, as we see in the various works of Ovid that were read and translated and imitated during the period. With the troubadours and the *dolce styl nuovo* this conception of love was exalted to the position of holding that it may ennoble human character, and indeed that it is most at home in the noble heart. According to Christianity, human love between the sexes was consecrated in the sacrament of matrimony and is therefore, as with any other sacrament, the channel of divine grace. It is not, however, the highest form of devotion to which human beings

may aspire, since the love of God must naturally come first.
Within these limitations, therefore, love according to Christianity is never sinful. (When the Wife of Bath cries out
"Allas! allas! that evere love was synne" (D. 614), she is
speaking broadly.) Outside of matrimony if it is expressed
in passion, and if the individual yields to his passion, it may
have sinful effects. (The sin is not love, but lust — which is
really a sin against love. Also it is possible that certain indi-
viduals may have a vocation for a singlehearted devotion to
the love of God, and for them the sacrament of matrimony
becomes an inferior channel of grace or even an obstacle.
The world would probably have been the loser if St Bene-
dict or St Francis had married and settled down to quiet domestic living. This, however, is not to say that everyone has
a vocation of this kind; for in some cases an individual
through pride, fancying himself one of the great saints, may
aspire to the celibate life although he is not fitted for it.
Possible confusion in all this can lie, not in the theory —
which, right or wrong, is as clear as day — but in the individual's own decision as to where his own vocation is to
be found.

The *Troilus*, which actually presents a classical story in a
medieval setting, is perfectly clear on the same terms. The
hero and the heroine might have married, but they chose
not to; and against the Christian background they indubitably sinned, not in their love but in yielding to their passion.)
Their love on Christian terms is a potential good, but in the
technique of the Court of Love it becomes trivial and is betrayed. On the other hand, when Chaucer adjures young folk
to repair home "fro worldly vanitee" to the love of God, he

can hardly mean to advocate celibacy for everyone; the sacrament of matrimony is not wholly vanity according to Christian teaching. If it should be said, therefore, that the poem is written in praise of love one might not have to demur entirely; yet one must quite definitely understand that Courtly Love is not what is meant thereby. And even so we must observe that the emphasis of the poem falls more on the failure of Courtly Love than it does on the benefits received from love itself. Troilus is transformed for the better by his devotion to Criseyde, but after his downfall he sings another tune.

2

It is not commonly understood that (Criseyde sinned even before her infidelity.) Chaucer is avowedly a writer who prefers not to judge the lady, as temperamentally he is one who sees things with justice but does not condemn. Yet no writer who presents reality can evade a precise judgment of his characters unless he selects only an instant out of their lives to study. Development in successive episodes must in part be based on judgment. (Pandarus and Criseyde both show a full awareness of the social aspect of what they are about in moving toward the love-scene.) They are, as we are often told, fourteenth-century figures; they are taken up with Courtly Love; the background is Christian despite the pagan deities named, and that is why the love affair must be kept secret. Secrecy, although of course expedient when an injured husband was in the offing, was a tenet of the Court of Love partly because love *paramours* was a violation of Christian morality and it received therefore a social condemnation. It is kept in the *Troilus* even where the lover has nothing to fear from an outraged husband. Criseyde shows her awareness of the true nature of her case when she complains of Pandarus:

> "Allas! what sholden straunge to me doon,
> When he, that for my beste frend I wende,
> Ret me to love, and sholde it me defende."
>
> ii, 411–413.

She goes on to say that Pandarus would have had no mercy on her if she had given her love to Achilles or some other man. She is not here concerned with the violation of her widowhood or with the idea that her love will become generally known. And Pandarus himself, not a man of spiced conscience, has his own qualms:

> "And were it wist that I, thorugh myn engyn,
> Hadde in my nece yput this fantasie,
> To doon thi lust and holly to ben thyn,
> Whi, al the world upon it wolde crie,
> And seyn that I the werste trecherie
> Dide in this cas, that evere was bigonne,
> And she forlost, and thow right nought ywonne."
>
> iii, 274–280.

The root of the difficulty is not the exposure, but that anyone who knew of the amour would condemn Pandarus for leading the lovers into it. Pandarus has no doubts, and neither has Criseyde. True it is that except for questions of decorum Criseyde herself has little concern for what people think about morality. Moral issues play no part in her decision regarding her lover. But from the point of view of a Christian social order Criseyde would be judged, and she obviously knows what the judgment would be. For practical purposes what guides her is thought of the effect on her immediate happiness. Can she, dare she, take the risk? Well, as she says, —

> ". . . He which that nothing undertaketh
> Nothyng n'acheveth . . ."
>
> ii, 807–808.

Now this is exactly what Diomede says when later he comes a-wooing:

> "For he that naught n'asaieth, naught n'acheveth."
>
> v, 784.

This is one more of the astonishing parallels in the poem. Cressid and Diomede are well mated. The religion of Pandarus, Criseyde, and Diomede, has a ritual of utilitarian proverbs.

But Mr. Lowes has brilliantly maintained that Cressid's yielding to Troilus happened "al bisyde hire leve" (iii, 622) — as Chaucer says of the storm and of her consenting to stay at the house of Pandarus. In my opinion it is simply not so. She had choice in the matter of going to the house of Pandarus; she had choice as to whether she would admit Pandarus and later Troilus to her room; she had choice as to whether she would admit Troilus to her bed, and also as to whether, once he was there, she would stay there herself. The compulsion of circumstance varies in degree in each of these instances; but never in any of them is she completely subject to the moment. The degree of her consent is delicately managed, we admit, so that she has almost nothing to do. This is a method that suits her temperament admirably.

(She is given to fear; it is almost her dominating characteristic and it is based on her fundamental sense of insecurity and on her personal egoism.) On the other hand, when need is, she is quite explicit to Troilus as to her reasons for surrender; although her reasons differ amazingly from the considerations on which she actually pondered when facing her choice, yet she wants her lover at least to believe that she has given herself freely.

Criseyde's process in deciding to go to Pandarus's house is much like her acceptance of the letter from Troilus. If it is thrust into her bosom she will accept it — and read it. The first episode is a commentary on the later one. Pandarus knows his niece, and now that the time is ripe he has warned the lovers that he will arrange a meeting for them at his house:

> "But I conjure the, Criseyde, and oon,
> And two, thow Troilus, whan thow mayst goon,
> That at myn hous ye ben at my warnynge,
> For I ful well shal shape youre comynge."
>
> iii, 193–196.

From his management of the meeting at the house of Deiphebus a timid girl might have suspected that Pandarus would accomplish this somewhat as a surprise; certainly anyone as shrewd as Criseyde shows herself to be in those marvelous interchanges of undeceiving deception between uncle and niece. She might even expect that in the later meeting with Troilus there would be a parallel to the elaborate story of Poliphete's conspiracy (for which the discussion was held), and she would not be disappointed; for we now have the elaborate lie about Horaste. And if Criseyde felt any interest

in Troilus, she would be a little stupid if she did not look
forward to some move of this sort on the part of her uncle.
Now as a matter of fact, as the scene develops, she shows
definitely that she has been looking for it. Pandarus offers his
invitation; Criseyde at once suggests that it is going to rain
and is doubtful about going. Pandarus presses his request
more urgently, whereupon Criseyde

> . . . gan to hym to rowne,
> And axed hym if Troilus were there.
>
> iii, 568–569.

Her uncle swears that the young man will not be there; indeed Pandarus wouldn't have the fellow seen there.

> Nought list myn auctour fully to declare
> What that she thoughte whan he seyde so,
> That Troilus was out of towne yfare,
> As if he seyde therof soth or no . . .
>
> iii, 575–578.

Can anyone miss the peculiarly Chaucerian quality of this
passage? Of course the poet leaves the question open. One
must read the lady's mind for oneself. How can the author
pry into it? Criseyde accepts, yes,

> But natheles, yet gan she hym biseche,
> Although with hym to gon it was no fere,
> For to ben war of goosish poeples speche,
> That dremen thynges whiche that nevere were . . .
>
> iii, 582–585.

But she wants to be sure that all is well:

> And seyde hym, "Em, syn I most on yow triste,
> Loke al be wel, and do now as yow liste."
>
> iii, 587–588.

Even on the face of it her consent is here. Well, Pandarus was not born yesterday. He swears a great and complicated oath that she may trust him; knowing her uncle as she does, she can read enough in that protest. Everything follows as it should, the fates do their part, the rain comes down, and Cressid stays. I will concede, freely enough, that for us the rain may symbolize the pressure of natural forces operating in the world, and some of its steamy life urges the desire of the fair heroine. But it would be nearer the facts to say that Criseyde was almost deterred by the rain from going to meet her lover; that she went in spite of the downpour after she guessed that Troilus was indeed there.

Of this episode Mr. de Selincourt has observed that Pandarus "takes it for granted that fear of discovery is the reason for her reluctance; and in the end she consents to come, though she knows, of course, why she has been invited." Fear of discovery doubtless has something to do with it; but it is partly fear of discovery to herself. The bedroom scene is still another parallel, and shows her in the same light. She is a lady who wants to yield to destiny — and then to put the blame on destiny. If such were not the case she might have cut off all thought of her affair with Troilus long ago. Before this, we read, Troilus

> . . . say his lady somtyme, and also
> She with hym spak, whan that she dorst and leste;
> And by hire bothe avys, as was the beste,
> Apoynteden full warly in this nede,
> So as they durste, how they wolde procede.
>
> iii, 451–455.

But why does Chaucer give us all this elaborate account of the preparation for the meeting in such extraordinary detail? Why does not Criseyde make her own appointment and go torch in hand to meet her lover? Surely, when she kissed him at the house of Deiphebus, she had a notion of what was ahead. Without doubt the fine process of her yielding is as lovely to watch as it was delicious to Criseyde. But can anyone think that it exhibits merely the pressure of circumstance by which a wholly virtuous lady is reduced to submission? (Is Cressid the victim of one rainy night? Surely in that case it is dangerous for a girl to step forth without an eye to the weather!) The poem teaches at least that much. Why did Chaucer display with such care the details of her growing consent to come to supper in the first place if the simple fact is that she had no slightest suspicion of what was involved — and no responsibility in going? I am afraid that if Chaucer really meant us to think that Cressid is guilt-free he has managed it very badly: "It is," continues Mr. de Selincourt, "the picture, not of a coquette, but of a woman pitifully weak" — this with reference to her negotiations with Diomede, but it is the same lady now. When Troilus knelt at her bedside, she might have gathered about her the garments of maidenly reserve and adopted for the nonce something of "daunger" from the Court of Love. But Chaucer says that she seemed to forget discretion — he hardly knows why — and even kissed the young man:

> Kan I naught seyn, for she bad hym nought rise,
> If sorwe it putte out of hire remembraunce,
> Or elles that she took it in the wise
> Of dewete, as for his observaunce;

But wel fynde I she dede hym this plesaunce
That she hym kiste, although she siked sore,
And bad hym sitte adown withouten more.
                                    iii, 967–973.

To this again is parallel the later part of the episode when
Troilus has recovered from his swoon and lies in her bed:

... hire thoughte tho no fere,
Ne cause ek non, to bidde hym thennes rise.
                                    iii, 1144–1145.

Why should we rush in to judge, when the poet himself
hesitates? The fact is, however, that Chaucer never shows
any real doubts about his heroine's responsibility. The long
and complicated account of her slow yielding shows quite
definitely that in her hesitation she is actuated a little by the
principle of "daunger" or what a generation or so ago
might have called feminine modesty, and again a little more
by fear of discovery, and considerably by fear of the consequences to her happiness; and this in part has to do with public censure if she is found out.

Yet it may be asked whether her own indifference to moral
issues does not entirely exonerate her from guilt. She sees no
wrong involved in loving Troilus. "Such is the way of an
adulterous woman," says the *Book of Proverbs*, "she eateth,
and wipeth her mouth, and saith I have done no wicked-
ness." Criseyde is not adulterous, and she is aware that there
is something wrong about giving herself to her lover. She
once rebuked Pandarus, as we have seen, for counselling her
to love, when he should be the first to refuse her the privilege. Her indifference means simply that she intends to be a

law to herself, and that certainly does not excuse her. She knew the social standards of her time. Chaucer has not let himself waver for the moment and depict a heroine of pagan morality. That we find her charming and forgive her, that Chaucer himself finds her charming and rejoices in her love, does not bear on the question in the least. We hear her lovely banter with her uncle:

> "Fox that ye ben! God yeve youre herte kare!
> God help me so, ye caused al this fare. . . ."
> iii, 1565–1566.

But this is the same lady as that who later writes to Troilus the needless and cruel lie:

> ". . . I have ek understonde
> How ye ne do but holden me in honde."
> v, 1614–1615.

Her immediate disavowal of faith in this only poisons it the more. Doubtless she thinks she is tempering the accusation, but she has made it first. Incidentally the stanza has a light air of confusion which Criseyde often adopts. Despite her determination to think things clearly through, she is a little upset at times when she talks to others. She knows not what to say; what do they want of her? and so on. The parallel in this vein runs through the three scenes: that first of Pandarus's telling her of her new suitor; that again at the house of Deiphebus; and finally that of the night at the house of Pandarus:

> "Now em," quod she, "what wolde ye devise?
> What is youre reed I sholde don of this?"
> ii, 388–389.

"I! what?" quod she, "by God and by my trouthe,
I not nat what ye wilne that I seye."
                    iii, 120–121.

"I am, til God me bettre mynde sende,
At dulcarnoun, right at my wittes ende."
                    iii, 930–931.

It is the confusion of a lady who wishes someone else to
manage things and also to take the blame.

3

In some ways Chaucer's portrait of Troilus is the harshest
feature of the poem. We first see him strutting up and down
the temple, like a young blood in medieval St Paul's. His
arrogance, his sneers at lovers, his taunts, are harmless enough
in human terms. Physically he is well proportioned, well
knit, attractive to look at, and I cannot find that he exploits
his charms as Diomede so skilfully manages to do later. His
access of lover's malady, his pining in distress, all these symp-
toms are comprehensible enough. But there is little on the
other side to balance the unrelieved pathos of his rôle. Even
when he clips and kisses fair Criseyde there is little humor in
his speech; his face is filled with bliss rather than happiness.
As the successful lover, it is true, he is transformed outwardly for a while; he becomes the friendliest of fellows and
one could wish his achievement, however immoral, might
be prolonged because it so much improves his manners. But
in general his solemnity in contrast to the liveliness of Pandarus, his constant complaints against Fate or Fortune which
reach a climax in his involved and tortuous soliloquy, his

frequent laments, all offer a picture that suits too perfectly the long pathos of his betrayal. Unlike Chaucer's young Squire we do not hear him whistling or fluting all the day. The natural health of youth does not balance his moods.

Mr. Lewis has attempted to explain the picture on the ground that it is Chaucer's purpose to develop this theme of pathos. Pity, as we know from the poet's repeated expression of the sentiment, is an emotion of the noble heart. I must pause for a moment, therefore, to consider how much Chaucer seems to have enjoyed pathos for its own sake. He was, we know, fed on the sweet commiserations of Court of Love literature early in his career. Early he began the pathetic narratives which one day he assigned to the Monk in the pilgrimage. He was touched sufficiently by the adventures of Constance and Virginia to retell their sufferings. He liked the story of the little clergeoun enough to give it to the Prioress. Above all he cared to take over almost unchanged the spectacle of the "forpyned" Griselda, whose mission seems chiefly to stir the reader to lacrimose reflections on life and its tests. It has even been said that the luxury of this sort of grief dominated the poet's interest; that like Euripides, Dickens, and others who do not shy away from sentimental values, he sought the fount of pathos whenever possible. But I find the emotional effect in all his works rather different from sentimentality. The poet's irony does not exclude pity, but it suffuses and transmutes it, notably in the setting given to it in the story of Griselda with its Envoy. He turns the brief tragedies over to the Monk, whose piety is, we see, formed on that kind of pity, and the Host offers a salutary comment:

> ". . . pardee, no remedie
> It is for to biwaille ne compleyne
> That that is doon, and als it is a peyne,
> As ye han seyd, to heere of hevynesse."
>   B. 3974–3977.

The consequent sullen reply of the Monk shows that Chaucer knew what sentimentalism soured was like. The pathos of Constance, Virginia, and the little clergeoun, is not unrelieved for in these cases it takes on the serenity of virtue and the celestial. Rebellious grief might have appeared in the *Knight's Tale* in the death of Arcite, but there we know, by comparing the story with the *Teseide*, the poet has reduced the element of pathos and increased the touches of something very close to humor. I would not, of course, imply that Chaucer did not know the full meaning of genuine pity for suffering; his charitable outlook and his understanding of human nature belie the possibility. But long stretches of pathos for its own sake do not appear in his works and are certainly not characteristic of his genius.

What then is the artistic significance of the sad case of young Troilus? In the light of Pandarus's attitude, his ridicule and his exhortations to brace up, I hardly think the hero's complaints are meant to stir us deeply, at least in the first part of the poem. Later they have in one instance a lyric value, namely in the ode to the empty house after Cressid's departure: "O thow lanterne of which queynt is the light," "And farwel shryne, of which the seynt is oute!" (v, 540 ff.) These are good figures, and Wordsworth, moved by the poetry, modernized the whole passage. But it is the scene itself which inevitably carries the poetry with it. One thinks of a corresponding picture in Meredith's *Diana of the Crossways*: "There stood the house. Absolutely empty! thought Redworth. The sound of the gate-bell he rang was like an echo to him. The gate was unlocked. He felt a return of his queer churchyard sensation when walking up the garden-path, in the shadow of the house. . . . Anticipating the blank silence, he rang the house-bell. It seemed to set wagging a weariful tongue in a corpse. . . ." In this case the house was not really so deserted as it looked, but the effect is the same. It was only yesterday that Walter de la Mare wrote:

> "Is there anybody there?" said the Traveller,
> Knocking on the moonlit door . . .

and the phantom listeners in the lone house "Stood listening in the quiet of the moonlight." The very idea of the desolate house in the *Troilus* is a sufficient appeal to experience for us to lend a willing response. But one may compare for poignant effect the familiar stanzas in the seventh canto of *In Memoriam*:

> Dark house, by which once more I stand
>   Here in the long unlovely street,
>   Doors, where my heart was used to beat
> So quickly, waiting for a hand. . . .

Chaucer's lines on Cressid's empty house have a subtle variety in the quality of the vowel-sounds and in the rhythmic beat, but the scene is trivial compared with Tennyson's picture. We cannot forget that the lady in the *Troilus* has simply gone out of town and that she is shortly to take another lover. The pathos of young Troilus, I fear, lacks its full measure of dignity, and so I find it does again and again

until he is relieved of the burden of the flesh. Chaucer's fourteenth-century audience may have wept over the lover's
woe, but the poet himself clearly saw the drama from another
level, "In convers letyng everich element," a little lower than
the angels no doubt but at least as high as the eighth sphere.

But still we have not explained the meaning of the linked
pathos long drawn out of the hero's career. In order to understand it we must, I am convinced, judge his case in terms of
a creature of flesh and blood; and that I believe to be possible.
For no matter how far Chaucer utilized the conventional and
borrowed from sources, his characters are living and must be
so criticized. We have admitted that Troilus has been controlled by the tenets of the Court of Love; and in discussing
his winning of Cressid through the intermediary of Pandarus
modern critics have been inclined to exonerate him for his
ineffectual qualities by saying that he is a typical lover of the
Court of Love. The excuse will not serve. Troilus is a living
human being. As that of a youth distinguished in the wars,
athletic and virile, his desire for Criseyde should normally
call forth his manliness so that he would go straight after his
lady without waiting for some friend to help him out. No
matter how many treatises told him that as a convert to
Courtly Love he should lie for a time and wallow and weep
like Niobe the Queen, normally he could have endured no
such restrictions where the lady was free and accessible. Even
his shame at having to retract his sneers at love and lovers
could not have counted for much so long as his affair in any
case had to be conducted secretly. At most it would have
evoked a boyish grin and a little awkwardness. At the very
least he would have achieved an interview with his lady at

once if he had shown the usual responses to stimuli. But Troilus goes to bed and bursts into tears; he lets a friend drag the secret from him, manage his wooing, dictate his first letter, arrange the meetings, and finally push him into bed with his *amie* telling him not to faint this time! Now I maintain that Chaucer knew and liked young men. He must have known that a fellow of Troilus's healthy type would go after his own prey, and that such indeed was part of the joy of this game.

All the rules of Courtly Love in a thousand handbooks do not explain the hero's lassitude before his first union with the lady; nor does the form of the story in Boccaccio, which Chaucer might quite readily have changed (and often did change). It is the hypothesis of the story, yes, but how could any realistic writer leave it so? In the *Merchant of Venice, Hamlet*, and elsewhere Shakespeare found the hypothesis of his story difficult to manage realistically, but that was his task; in *Troilus and Cressida* he hurried over and avoided the full problem of Pandarus in this matter. The fact is that Troilus's habit of turning over his wooing to another man is in agreement with his nature all through Chaucer's story. Many readers have objected to his weakness in letting Cressid leave Troy; but he shows the same feature on that occasion. In terms of real life he wants to be in part controlled by circumstance, in part responsible; and in this he is like Criseyde. He is a good soldier, but again and again he shows a touch of fear as to what life will do for him. His soliloquy on predestination in Book IV is the perfect expression of his need to put the blame for failure on something outside himself. He shows a measure of what is nowadays called the will to fail-

ure, especially in his manner with Criseyde in the love-
scene:

> And in his mynde he gan the tyme acorse
> That he com there, and that he was born.
>
> iii, 1072–1073.

Such sentiments are only too familiar to the modern psychologist, who has a name for the emotion expressed herewith. And here we find the reason for his habitual trick of
not putting his best foot forward; it is like his "surrogation"
in taking emotional satisfaction through expressions of despair rather than through direct activity. In all this Diomede
is his complement, who wastes few words and little time.

Young people, I find, often ask why Criseyde was persuaded to leave Troy. They are not content with the answer
that the matter was settled by the vote of Parliament, or that
the heroine's timid nature led her to play safe on every occasion and therefore on this. And I think there is something
in their question. Why did she go after all? If she was satisfied with Troilus, why didn't she use one of the many resources at her command to stay longer in Troy with her
lover? She might have played sick, or she might have worked
on the sympathies of Troilus and Pandarus to help her resist
the mandate awhile. She was a clever woman, and she knew
it; but it is she who persuades Troilus that it is better for her
to go. I cannot help wondering whether in Troilus's lack of
real stamina (to draw it mild), the lack of forthright mas-
culinity, she was left a little unsatisfied, readier perhaps to
move elsewhere. She made no move after her union with
the stalwart Diomede (her excuses, v, 694 ff., mean noth-

ing) — or before it — to use her resources to return to Troy or even to visit the city again.

I know we shall be told that all this is rank modernism, reading into Chaucer's poem ideas that the poet simply could not have imagined. The technique of Courtly Love, critics will say, explains all this. But they forget that the realistic genius of the poet would hardly accept a convention he could not vitalize; and here enters the problem of living human nature as it is now as well as it has been, with all the characteristics so plain to psychological study as well as with mysteries yet unsolved. But, someone may object, Aurelius in the *Franklin's Tale* keeps his love secret for a long time; is he another example of this type? Aurelius, we must remember, was in a different situation; for he was in love with another man's wife, while Criseyde was a widow. Furthermore he did speak to his lady as soon as he dared. Can we suppose that young lovers in the Middle Ages were really restrained by directions in some code of manners on the subject? Not if they had nerve. In any case, the examples of a dozen lovers who hid their devotion would not account for the fact that Troilus lets Pandarus accomplish almost everything for him. It is an extraordinary phenomenon that Chaucer must have faced. His solution of the problem was to show the hero as generally disinclined to dominate the situation, to accept full responsibility. And in harmony with this we find Troilus at the very start jeering at love and lovers. What is the significance of that in modern psychology? It shows him again personally insecure, personally unwilling to take the risk of a venture in love; and so by way of compensation he jeers at the whole business and thus protects his *amour propre*. But why should the young man have felt any insecurity in such matters — was he not fully alive and normal, as competent as any young Trojan? Into this question the poet was not compelled to enter, even if he had thought of it. His creation he made without the benefit of modern psychology, but with that intuitive understanding of life and human beings that marks him among the greatest. Troilus in his fears is a balance to Cressid and her timidity; they are both a foil to the rashly confident Pandarus, whose guidance brings them all to failure, and to the sanely confident Diomede, who gets what he wants. Again the symmetry of the poem is made clear, and again we see its perfection of detail.

So when the stricken Troilus, alone in the temple, looks upon himself and curses his fate, we are not, I think, expected to weep with him. Least of all are we expected to be taught wisdom by his wild and whirling words —

> "For if ther sitte a man yond on a see
> Than by necessite bihoveth it
> That, certes, thyn opynyoun sooth be,
> That wenest or conjectest that he sit.
> And further over now ayeynward yit,
> Lo, right so is it of the part contrarie. . ."
>
> iv, 1023–1028.

"furthermore nevertheless notwithstanding however" — indeed how can anyone have ever thought so! For if Geoffrey Chaucer shows himself at all in his works, he shows himself a healthy spirit. And I hear his voice when Pandarus comes in upon the woeful Troilus and says: "I! who say evere a wis man faren so?" (iv, 1087.)

But in stating all this I would not maintain that our hero is one-sided or somewhat pathological. His vitality shows itself when he takes out his rebelliousness in battling with the Greeks. His exultant heart produces not only poetry but song. His excellent naïveté appears in his grateful willingness to procure his sister for Pandarus. His burst of temper is wholly refreshing. It breaks as happily into the monotony of his despair at Cressid's going, as Griselda's momentary concern that Walter shall not "torment" the new bride interrupts her own continued "sadnesse" (stability). Says the angry Troilus:

> "O oold, unholsom, and mislyved man,
> Calkas I mene, allas! what eileth the,
> To ben a Grek, syn thow art born Troian?
> O Calkas, which that wolt my bane be,
> In corsed tyme was thow born for me!
> As wolde blisful Jove, for his joie,
> That I the hadde, wher I wolde, in Troie!"
>
> iv, 330–336.

He not only puts the blame on Calkas for his own misadventure, but according to his regular practise he explains Calkas and his sins by external circumstance. Another outburst shows his trick of turning on everybody except himself; Cassandra has interpreted his dream to his own disadvantage:

> "Thow seyst nat soth," quod he, "thow sorceresse.
> With al thy false goost of prophecye!
> Thow wenest ben a gret devyneresse!"
>
> v, 1520 ff.

And so on. "You think you are a great seer, you do!" It is the living voice with the accent of youth! But Chaucer himself has not joined in the spleen any more than he does in the hero's desperate explication of the doctrine of necessity. Why speak out? No one can tell this turbulent young soul anything. He must come to his own clarification, and he does when Achilles gives him the *coup de grâce*. We follow his spirit up to the hollowness of the eighth sphere, to a pinnacle of enlightenment once enjoyed by Scipio Africanus, the soul of Pompey, and Boccaccio's disappointed Arcite. Youth and Courtly Love and pathos itself look different against the background of eternity.

4

The character of Pandarus has more tang than any other in the poem. Diomede, of course, is a healthier person; but Pandarus's old griefs, his frustrations, have given him a kind of oblique wisdom about life that, while it does not carry anything through to a perfect finish, supplies certain amenities *en route*. His humor would, I am sure, be a fatal astringent if it were not for his affections. He loves Troilus and he is fond of his niece, and his joking if a little acid is kindly. Furthermore he knows something about human nature. Diomede's swift approach is really made possible through Pandarus's earlier success; and that was based on a skilful, unerring as well as gradual, procedure. Pandarus has indeed been called the real hero of the poem; and, while the notion ignores the emphasis in the material, there is just a little to be said for it. He too has meddled in the affairs of Courtly Love; he too has paid and is paying his fee therefore. His own tragedy runs along in the undertone of casual reference, sometimes in a recurrent family joke used by Criseyde for purposes of social distraction and sometimes in the solemn charge of Troilus that his friend hardly knows the game. It is an obligato to the main theme, touching it with irony when in spite of Pandarus's achievement with the lovers the end is not joy. But Pandarus has yet another form of tragedy that comes closer to him and indeed forms part of the main interest of the story.

Even before our plot begins he has suffered in love, and now he turns to meddle with love *paramours* in a different way. He has not been able to reach satisfaction with his own lady; he is no longer young; and his energies must have some other outlet. Why did he fail in his earlier exploit? There are a dozen possible explanations; and one that critics might suggest is that he is cynical, and his cynicism did not spring from his ill-success but was the cause of it. It was his own type of despair that brought its own negation. Yet all this is unlikely; for he is not deeply cynical except, as Mr. Kittredge remarks, in "the turn of his epigrams." On the contrary he shows an astounding faith in love *paramours*, even in the value of the chase. Through his friendship with Troilus he finds an opportunity for exercising his creative powers in a conspiracy the like of which he had seemingly not attempted before. He is to bring his friend to a gratification of passion. His imagination, his humor, his diplomacy, and his cunning, are all called upon, first to insinuate the idea of love into the mind of his niece and then to manage a part of the wooing. To the whole task he brings an immense vigor in the name of friendship. What satisfaction he anticipated in the relief to Troilus's own desires it is difficult to estimate. His affection for the hero seems to be normally robust; he rumples his friend and drags the truth out of him. But his pursuit of Criseyde and his machinations seem to have a fervor that harks back to his failure to win another lady for himself.

In fact he seems to take out his frustration in his excitement at his present success. His is a passionate nature, although his passion is often sublimated in jests at his own expense and in generous activity. He stops at nothing, and when he makes a gain he is jubilant. When he gets Criseyde to the point of asking whether her suitor talks well of love, he smiles a little at the symptom and gives an elaborate and (it would seem) wholly fictitious account of Troilus's recantation of his old error. He identifies himself with the hero in his desperate need of the lady's pity. She will slay them both if she does not relent. He is deeply moved with sympathy for the lover; he is all on the *qui vive* to achieve the first meeting. It is he who tells the lover how to write his first letter, and how to act at the house of Deiphebus. Once there, when Troilus makes his plea, Pandarus

> . . . wep as he to water wolde,
> And poked evere his nece new and newe.
> iii, 115-116.

When Criseyde at last kisses her lover, Pandarus is lyrically beside himself:

> Fil Pandarus on knees, and up his eyen
> To heven threw, and held his hondes highe,
> "Immortal god," quod he, "that mayst nought deyen,

Cupid I mene, of this mayst glorifie;
And Venus, thow mayst maken melodie!
Withouten hond, me semeth that in towne,
For this merveille, ich here ech belle sowne."
iii, 183–189.

We might take all this as only a part of the energetic nature he always displays, and there would be a portion of truth
in the contention. But that is not all there is to it. On the
night at his house when Troilus faints, he pushes the hero
into Cressid's bed and strips off his clothes. At all times he
shows a great concern lest a false move be made; an artist
could not take more excessive pains. While the lovers talk,
he stands by as if to superintend their *rapprochement*; and he
does not settle down to his own rest until Troilus has actually taken his lady in his arms. One may see something in all
this to Troilus's discredit, as we follow the swiftly developing drama, and thus one may lose pleasure in the lovers' con-
summation of their bliss; but our attention is given partly to
the masterful achievement of Pandarus, and so the final disaster in the story does not frustrate a sense of perfect lovers
brought into union. For they are not perfect or anything like
it; and we do not feel injured at Pandarus's fling: "Swouneth
nought now, lest more folk arise!" (iii, 1190.) When a young
man has had as much opportunity as Troilus did, one might
think that his good friend could have left the reins to him
somewhat earlier. It is as if Pandarus were determined that
the hero should not fail in his part; he does everything but
carry it out for him. And next day when Pandarus makes fun
of his niece, asking in Byronic fashion if the rain let her sleep
(where incidentally the allusion emphasizes the setting), he

almost seems to check up on the episode to be certain. He will not permit failure. Emotionally if not intellectually he must be sure. Now we perceive the gusto in his ironic speech the evening before: "And if ye liggen wel to-nyght, com ofte!" (iii, 669.) And he does arrange the further meetings.

So in his way Pandarus meddles with the affairs of love. Thus he too becomes involved in the central theme of the poem, and like the others he has his tragedy. For as the story proceeds he becomes steadily less and less effective, and at the last he is a futile and pathetic figure, no comfort to Troilus and under the charge of being the source of all the young man's woe. The high point for Pandarus comes just before the meeting of the lovers at his house, when he gives Troilus a full statement of his own position and some candid advice. Here is Pandarus at his best; here he is wholly admirable:

> " . . . for the am I bicomen
> Bitwixen game and ernest, swich a meene
> As maken wommen unto men to comen;
> Al sey I nought, thow wost wel what I meene.
> For the have I my nece, of vices cleene,
> So fully maad thi gentilesse triste,
> That al shal ben right as thiselven liste."
>
> iii, 253–259.

In this speech he is perfectly honest. He can afford to be, doubtless: he is in a point of vantage with respect to his friend, his niece, and circumstance, and he certainly feels secure. Troilus reminds him that this love affair is on a higher level than that of harlotry; but they both know that what Pandarus is up to will not bear public scrutiny, and that it is no theme for glory however much they enjoy it. Pandarus makes clear the nature of his own sacrifice to his friend, and there is an interchange of affection between them which reaches its fulfilment in the satisfaction later to the passions of Troilus. There seems to be no trace of compromise in Troilus's high regard for him at this moment.

Then comes the downfall. When Cressid must leave Troy, Pandarus can really do nothing about it. Extraordinarily skilful as he has been with fate and friends, his powers fail him now. His advice to keep the lady somehow by force may be sound enough; but Troilus feels the suggestion should be referred to Criseyde. It is strange to find Pandarus so much at a loss as to counsel his friend to take another lady:

> "And over al this, as thow wel woost thiselve,
> This town is ful of ladys al aboute;
> And, to my doom, fairer than swiche twelve
> As evere she was, shal I fynde in som route,
> Yee, on or two, withouten any doute.
> Forthi be glad, myn owen deere brother!
> If she be lost, we shal recovere an other."
>
> iv, 400–406.

Quack, said the duck, there are more stars, God knows, than a pair! Thus Juliet's nurse offered advice to her stricken mistress when fate looked unfavorable. Of course, Pandarus was not entirely serious; Chaucer sympathetically tells us that. He only wanted to comfort Troilus. But the point is that he didn't know what else to say. And what is more, his advice at every point lacks the old certainty. He will help the fellow to retain his lady by violence, will fight in the streets for him, but he has the fatally poor judgment to add that as Paris had an *amie* so Troilus is entitled to one:

"Thenk ek how Paris hath, that is thi brother,
A love; and whi shaltow nat have another?"
iv, 608–609.

This serves again to tie up the affair of Troilus with the Fate
of Troy itself: if ever a love-affair *paramours* was punished by
the gods the rape of Helen was, and the results are all about
them. Further on, Pandarus has the bad grace to suggest,
if ever so slightly, the possibility that Cressid may be
unfaithful:

"And if she wilneth fro the for to passe,
Thanne is she fals; so love hire wel the lasse."
iv, 615–616.

No doubt his manner is eagerly reassuring, but this is cold
comfort. Later we come to the scene when hero and heroine
are reunited to talk it over: Cressid faints, and Troilus,
thinking she is dead, is about to commit suicide but being
Troilus has to make a speech to Jove and Fortune and others
first. The scene is a parallel and counterpart to their first
night together when the hero fainted. What might have
ended with the splendor of *Romeo and Juliet*, however, here
fades almost into bathos; the lovers are soon found discussing
the question of stealing away together. Criseyde dominates
the situation, Troilus yields, and they comfort each other
with love. But this time there is no roguish word from a
triumphant Pandarus to cheer them. The humor of this
good friend now has another turn. Later follows the scene
in which he goes with Troilus to see the empty house; he is
the youth's constant companion, he waits with him for
Cressid at the gates; and he utters lying words of hope:

> But in his herte he thoughte, and softe lough,
> And to hymself ful sobreliche he seyde,
> "From haselwode, there joly Robyn pleyde,
> Shal come al that that thow abidest heere.
> Ye, fare wel al the snow of ferne yere!"
>
> v, 1172–1176.

The laugh of Pandarus is no longer pleasant. It is a bitter fool!

If Troilus is constantly pathetic, so Pandarus continues to be futile in whatever he does. He tries in vain to deceive the young man about the meaning of his dream; he tries to stop the poor fellow's tears; and, as at first, he counsels him to write to Criseyde. But Troilus at length sees his brooch on the collar of Diomede's coat and knows the truth. In a convulsion of feeling he turns to his friend and says: "O Pandarus, now canst thou see how true is thy niece!" And this versatile gentleman for once is left without a word — as still as a stone. When at length he does speak, it sounds like defense:

> "My brother deer, I may do the namore.
> What sholde I seyen? I hate, ywys, Cryseyde;
> And, God woot, I wol hate hire evermore!
> And that thow me bisoughtest don of yoore,
> Havyng unto myn honour ne my reste
> Right no reward, I dide al that the leste."
>
> v, 1731–1736.

Pandarus is usually an adult, having derived from sufferings in love now freely accepted a maturity that Troilus lacks. But there is a childish element in this speech: I hate Cressid and I always shall hate her; you got me into this, Troilus, and I was very unselfish about it too, doing anything you wanted me to do! The mood is like that of Troilus's recrimination — for the hero by implication puts the blame on Pandarus — and the speeches balance each other. But more than all this, we cannot help realizing that Pandarus too feels betrayed, and the infidelity touches him as well as his friend. If he could mend things, he would gladly do so, but may Criseyde soon die! "I kan namore seye."

There is still beauty, if you like, in his persistent loyalty to the young hero, which follows along during the weeks or months of waiting for the lady's return and furnishes a living contrast to her perfidy. But even this suffers injury in the outcome. Pandarus thought he had taken many a risk and sacrificed much for Troilus, but it was only to have their friendship marred. And Troilus does not give a happy appearance when he turns on the older man with reproach for lack of trust in the dream that exposed the truth of the matter. It is with the general failure of Pandarus that Shakespeare ends his play: "Ignomy and shame," says the hero to his old friend, "Pursue thy life and live aye with thy name!" (V, x, 33–34.) "Swich fyn hath his noblesse!"

"Ah! *Vanitas Vanitatum!* which of us is happy in this world? Which of us has his desire? or, having it, is satisfied? — Come, children, let us shut up the box and the puppets, for our play is played out." Or are they puppets quite? When Thackeray wrote these words, did he mean that Becky Sharp was an innocent creature beleaguered by heritage and circumstance? No, his judgment in her case is clear; and so it is with Chaucer in respect to Troilus and Cressida and Pandarus. Hell-mouth yawns, but nobody is bad enough to go there so far as we know. We do not care, however, to fol-

low Criseyde too long with our eyes. Henryson later had his
thoughts of what happened to her, although he tried his best
to exonerate her of guilt; and it was from his poem that the
tradition sprang that named her the "lazar kite." But our
question here is whether the story Chaucer presents is a unit
in all its parts with all its changes and additions including the
Epilogue. According to our present reading it is closely knit;
and whatever condemnations appear at the end, they are implicit in the whole poem. When we see how the structure
holds together — so that motivation is supplied before and
even after an event (as when Pandarus reflects, i, 908 ff., on
the old days in which Troilus scorned love) — how its symmetry has an almost logical precision, how the parallelism in
the large and in detail builds up the irony, and how the
philosophical passages from Boethius harmonize with the
drama and with the general sense of the poem, it is hard to
imagine that its author was careless about its meaning. At the
beginning of the story the poet says:

> Refuseth nat to Love for to ben bonde,
> Syn, as hymselven liste, he may yow bynde.
>   i, 255–256.

At the end we find the exclamation, "Lo here, thise wrecched
worldes appetites" (v, 1851). Are these passages incompati-
ble? Love itself is not what the poet means by "appetite."
Surely in the first Chaucer is touching lightly on human
frailty just as at the end he bears down with more force
upon his theme. Take this book, O moral Gower, and thou,
O philosophical Strode! It is moral enough! It would be
stultifying indeed to suppose that in the dedication Chaucer

really meant a taunt because he knew his book was actually immoral, or because he thought it a sentimental blast against cruel Fate cloaked in a pretense of orthodoxy at the end, or — saddest possibility of all since it has a modern ring — because he thought his story rose above all moral considerations. The poem is not divided, nor was the poet himself. If we know anything about Geoffrey Chaucer at all, it is certain that he was integrated, that in a word his outlook is characterized by health. We find soundness in his constant humor, which is his sanity.

Chapter IV

TROILUS ON DETERMINISM

WORDS are often flung about in critical usage, until a few of them stick to a subject and grow there like barnacles, as if their attachment were foreordained and their appropriateness inevitable. Thus in regard to Chaucer's interest in fatalism the word "determinism" has more and more crept into use with reference to his thought, and even Price remarks of the famous soliloquy of Troilus that it has a "special interest in showing us the settled determinism of Chaucer's philosophical conception of human life." When so significant an expression is used so often it must be scrutinized afresh, first for its own meaning in the modern vernacular, and secondly for its accuracy in describing the poet's philosophical ideas.

The need for such a word arises when we try to indicate the stages in the theoretical relation between the opposite poles of human freedom and external compulsion or necessity. What appears to be its readiest implication is that of the extreme of absolute compulsion — "determinism," when you look at it, is after all a hard word, — and, in fact, that is the usual meaning attached to it to-day. If it is used to connote only a degree of compulsion, then it loses in definiteness; for nearly everybody, the orthodox Christian, the pagan, the modern scientist, everyone but an out and out libertarian (as the Pelagians do vainly talk), would be a determinist. There are other terms to cover the fact of some external influence in human life, and we need one which excludes the theory of any trace of free will. In this essay, then, I shall confine the use of "determinism" and allied expressions to such a meaning. I shall consider whether in this sense it has any applicability to the views expressed in Chaucer's *Troilus,* and what conclusions may be drawn regarding the poet's own ideas on the subject. First it will clarify the situation to look briefly into the discussion of the subject during the Middle Ages as a background to the poet's theory.

I

The importance of the question in literary history is not only intellectual but aesthetic. In literature artistic appeal varies in depicting, on the one hand, a character moved entirely by what amount to external forces (whether heritage, humors, or motives over which the individual has no control), and, on the other, a character morally responsible because, in part at least, free to choose his course. Without raising the issue of art for art's sake, we may note that in this sense the values of a work of art may include moral patterns as well as others, and that the emotional response may be changed by the fact that the onlooker cannot put aside the situation as in any way isolated, or as unrelated to his own action in the future. Reflection may be added to pity and terror if one has the conviction that one can affect one's own destiny in part, and that the future is something more than a question of mere luck. In comparison, an entirely fatalistic tragedy seems less rich in variety, and to many will appear even warped as a picture of life. With such an art as that of fatalism there is nothing to do but weep. But whether the experience of moral tragedy is salutary or not, we may observe that it is different in important ways from that received at the spectacle of the action of irresponsible puppets.

The aesthetic importance of the distinction was clearly perceived by Aristotle, who, in discussing tragedy, at first points out that for hero an entirely virtuous man will not do, for his adversity will merely shock us. On the other hand, in what is really an inductive fashion, inferring his principles from the drama of his day, and trying to formulate them in relation to his philosophy, Aristotle traces the development of a tragedy to an essential weakness in the hero. This, it is true, need not be a moral weakness, but there can be little doubt that Aristotle deliberately chose the inclusive expression ἁμαρτία because he was giving special attention to his favorite tragedy, the *Oedipus Tyrannus*. For elsewhere in his works the necessity of moral responsibility and of moral value is never ignored, and he shows definitely his belief in an element of human free will. The gravity of the question, however, is reflected in the discussion among critics as to the precise meaning of ἁμαρτία and as to the real cause of the tragedy in the story of Oedipus. For the latter, Professor Abby Leach has maintained, with apparent justice, that even there a moral weakness furnishes the spring to the action: "Yet Sophocles plainly shows even in his case that his own traits of character brought on and augmented the catastrophe. Further, this play is but one. . . ." And of the characteristics of the Greeks the same writer remarks: "Freedom of thought, freedom of action, love of the beautiful, joy in living, incessant activity . . . all these are diametrically opposed to any fatalistic doctrine, to anything bordering on patient and unquestioning submission to the fixed and unalterable decrees of fate." While the Greeks had a sense of destiny, they were able to sustain the paradox of fate and free will, so well recognized and discussed in the Middle Ages. The critic's enthusiasm shows the instinctive revolt almost anyone feels at any kind of moral slavery.

The fact that Aristotle puts the cause of real tragedy in a flaw, moral or otherwise, in the leading character, rather than in the crushing power of more purely external circumstance, suggests that his own preference was typically humanistic — that he held that character, rather than forces outside the individual, is destiny. By this we cannot mean that character is only another variety of destiny (inasmuch as character is partly a gift of nature); for it is an impressive fact that Aristotle does not put the prime cause in outer nature or in the plans of the gods. The whole point of the ἀμαρτία is not that it is the necessary hypothesis for destruction, but that it brings the one touch of human nature in which we may resemble the hero and apply his case to ours and ours to his. We may have tragedies where the whole action is concerned with the helpless destruction of a group of beings, where every cause is external, where no gesture or action springs from a vital spark of freedom, and thus where all the lines of artistic appeal form a beautiful harmony in their direction downward like a soft shower. The cross currents introduced by the interplay of free motivation will be lacking. But such tragedies will represent the sort·of art left to us when the pseudo-scientist and certain psychological faddists have done their worst with human nature, and they will really embody determinism. Such, however, is not the tragedy of the Greeks, where irony springs from the reality of the human will striving in conflict with and sometimes playing into the hands of fate. Even if one holds that the human will always succumbs in any conflict with fate, and thus produces a sentimental philosophy of pessimism, the result will be other than deterministic. On the other hand, to maintain that on certain occasions the will is of no avail, and that occasionally the innocent suffer, is a still different conception. Such, I believe, is the view of Sophocles.

The real difficulty in dealing with the problem of fatalism in art comes from the fact that the mind is likely to reject the paradox of fate and free will as a contradiction. When the element of fate in a plot is successfully demonstrated, one may rush to the conclusion that free will is excluded. But the Greeks retained some belief in both; and the Middle Ages, from St Augustine and Boethius on, kept the same tradition in their analysis of predestination or grace and their recurrent insistence on human freedom and moral responsibility. Yet the difficulty in keeping a balance between the ideas appears in the medieval debate and modern accounts of it. Thus St Thomas Aquinas follows the Aristotelian tradition of making the will subject, in a sense, to the intellect; so much so that Windelband, writing of the Occamist and Thomist controversy, speaks of St Thomas's view as that of "intellectualistic determinism." Now I suppose that to-day no one would seriously maintain that in the ordinary sense of the word Thomas Aquinas was really a determinist. The great Doctor certainly held that, where knowledge is clear, choice will move immediately to what is best. But in actual fact knowledge is seldom so clear, and rarely is full freedom of that kind made our own (until the Truth makes us free). For the present argument it is sufficient to bear in mind that St Thomas allows choice between differing values; and one may further consult his argument that man does not choose of necessity, and read again his sections on the goodness of the will, on merit and demerit.

The solution of the problem lies partly in the fact that man may suffer worldly tragedy and yet, like Job, win spiritual victory. This to some will be as unsatisfactory as the spiritual reward seems unreal; and for a valid free will they may insist that the human will should have power to control material destiny, although that is another matter. Boethius resolves the difficulty by putting the whole question where it belongs — in eternity, where Divine foresight is unlimited, and parallel lines are at last to meet. It is thither, we recall, that after his debate on fate and free will the soul of Troilus takes its flight.

2

From the present discussion of the paradox it is obvious that in considering Chaucer's ideas of determinism, heaping up instances of his apparent fatalism is a futile task. The gods rule the story of Palamon and Arcite as they rule life in general; astronomical forces touch the life of Constance; and we know from the discussion of God's prescience in Boethius that any man's death is "shapen" ere his "sherte." But we lose enormously in appreciating Chaucer if we assume that because "it is one of the glories of Chaucer's tragic art that he should have dignified his drama of human experiences by linking them up with those more mysterious and awe-inspiring forces of destiny which govern both men and the universe," he has therefore eliminated the meaning and artistic value of human free will. In the *Knight's Tale*, Chaucer has taken pains to draw on Boethius for his references to chance, and, as I have shown elsewhere, has gone out of his way *for some reason or other* to reproduce the Christian portrait of Fortune in Dante in his own account of Destiny — Destiny who carries out the "purveiaunce" of God, which, as any reader of Boethius knows, cannot and does not affect the power of human free will. Furthermore, when Arcite suffers, we remember that it was in defiance of his oath of brotherhood that he turned rival to Palamon, who after all (and it is another of Chaucer's alterations) was the first to see the lady. The gods themselves are indeed for a time doubtful about the issue. Whatever the degree of sentimentalism in the story told by Boccaccio, Chaucer has gone to the trouble of restoring "poetic justice," and, though a sense of proportion would keep one from pressing too hard the element of moral responsibility in a story of this kind, if this is a case of determinism then it is the most flexible and gentle determinism known to man.

It is a ponderous business to analyze these tales for moral implications; but it is only by so doing that we can get a hint of the author's point of view. The same difficulty rises in discussing the *Troilus*, which is a poem of youth written with incomparable lightness and charm. In dealing with it, however, we are bound to observe that, whatever the poet's joy in the telling, he has not taken the composition lightly;

and a point of cardinal importance for penetrating to his own
ideas is the necessity of comparing the poem with its sources
for evidence of the nature of the changes introduced. One
might have supposed that this was somewhat axiomatic in
the field of scholarship to-day. The important elements in
these changes (in comparison with the *Filostrato*), often noted
before, are chiefly directed toward a deep intensification of
the values which Chaucer found in his original. This is true,
whether it is a question of the subtlety of Criseyde and her
candor with herself, or the physical details of the love-affair.
Pandarus is set more in contrast to Troilus because he is
older, and achieves a special individuality thereby; and his
function thus becomes the clearer, and in more perfect harmony with his vicarious satisfaction in the success of Troilus,
and with his futility when Criseyde is faithless. Diomede as
well is more Diomede than ever, when (as in Benoit) he
makes love to Criseyde at once on her return instead of later.
And finally the element of fate is dignified by additions from
Boethius on the philosophical side, and deepened by astrological material. These additions might lead one to regard the
poem as a study of a particular case of the slings and arrows of
outrageous Fortune.

But one must not overdo the matter. While character,
love, and the "influences of these hevenes hye," and fate
itself in various ways, affect the actions of the characters in
the poem, we can hardly have a right to put all these elements together, as merely separate aspects of destiny, to show
the total effect of destiny on the reader or hearer. Some
theorizers, it is true, did analyze fate or fortune into such
separate manifestations; but we cannot assume that the aver-

age reader could be relied upon to perform the reverse process, to achieve the synthesis of all these various things, and thus to read into the poem an overwhelming power of fate which would make unreal a single stirring of merely human impulse. Few readers, I think, would see in Troilus's impulse to love the same force as that which ruled the doom of Troy. Moreover, the great majority of Chaucer's references to Fortune or Fate are based on similar passages in the *Filostrato*, and there the same fatal scheme is in process. But even if Chaucer wanted to pile Ossa upon Pelion in his attempt to increase the brooding sense of fate, yet, as we have seen, medievally he may not have had the slightest intention of excluding human free will. Most of his additions on the subject are taken from the argument of Boethius, and yet the conclusion of that argument in what is almost his "favorite book" is a defense of free will. What more could fate do against Boethius, and yet what else do we learn in the *Consolatio* but the power of man in spite of odds? There is no more in the *Troilus* on the subject of destiny, astrology, or the grace of God than in the *Divine Comedy*, and yet Dante's poem is chiefly occupied with the expectations of moral responsibility.

But we do not have to concede so much as all that. At least three times Chaucer has taken pains to show his own point of view by departing from his source in passages carefully made to reveal what he thought. These resemble in some respects the corresponding passages in the *Knight's Tale* and his full discussion in the *Balade* on Fortune. If ever a writer expressed clearly and emphatically what he thought in such a case, Chaucer most certainly did. In the famous soliloquy of Troilus in Book IV, the hero gives, it is true, considerable expression to what, for the sake of the argument, we may call determinism — although I think he is rather complaining against predestination and trying to exonerate himself without impiety. In any case, there is no reason to suppose that this monologue is spoken for other than dramatic effect. It shows the youth in a typical mood, giving way to his feelings rather than to his intellect, with all the solemnity of his despair in a situation on which the poem as a whole sheds ironic light. In the three passages referred to, however, Chaucer deliberately modifies the philosophy of the story he found in Boccaccio, giving definite expression to a Christian point of view — in two, adopting from Boethius and Dante the description of a Christian Fortuna (iii, 617 ff. and v, 1541 ff.), which removes the element of caprice from destiny, and restores the control to a rational rather than an arbitrary God; and in the third, the Epilogue, expressly interpreting the whole plot on Christian terms. It was unnecessary to call on Boethius and Dante for the idea of Fortune as subservient to God, if the story was simply one of disaster and fatalism; the two passages are in harmony with the third, which they precede and interpret. Moreover the two passages occur at the crises of the plot, and with the third at the end bind the philosophical construction of the plot together. Thus, for anyone who reads the story as Chaucer wrote it, there is no break between the early part where Troilus gives himself up a willing victim to the Court of Love, and the end where he sees that in his tragedy were the elements of folly and learns that he has suffered from the consequences of his own choice. Of the Epilogue Professor

Root has finely said: "Yet it is no mere tacked-on moral. It is implicit in the whole poem. . . . Chaucer is not so much pointing a moral, as giving us at the end his own verdict as to the permanent values of those aspects of our human life which are for the moment of such passionate importance."

Here is the mainspring of the tragedy, and here is the answer to Troilus's own soliloquy and modern assumptions of determinism in the poem. To take the words of Professor Curry: ". . . . the man who does not exercise his free-will in the control and direction of his emotions, finds himself presently without free-choice in the guidance of his actions when the power of the stars descends upon him or when he comes in contact with the destinal force inherent in other people's influence." That is well put, except that we must note that the point of choice for the man comes when he "does not exercise his free-will." One would suppose, however, that the three important additions to the poem were sufficiently clear indications of Chaucer's own ideas, written with the greatest care, darting here for a word and there for a phrase, and finally putting the whole matter as forcibly and beautifully as ever the conclusion of a poem could. If we leave out passages like these because they conflict with our theories, we may read the *Consolation of Philosophy* as a fine study of settled determinism, and the *Divine Comedy* as a superb pagan tragedy.

3

Let us waive all previous argument, however, and try to imagine that the *Troilus* was meant to embody determinism. What then would be its meaning? In the first place, much of the criticism of the poem written so far must be discarded as worthless. Thus when Mr. Kittredge observes of Criseyde, "She soon discovers that she has matched her woman's wit, not against her dotard father merely, but against the doom of Troy," we realize that she has done nothing of the kind. Nature-as-Destiny has given her the woman's wit, and the stars have given her the impulse to match it against the doom of Troy. Hers is a case of Fate against Fate, nothing less and nothing more. When Mr. Curry remarks of Troilus, "He fights at first against the destinal powers that would give him Criseyde for a season; he struggles against the forces which would finally take her away from him" — (an acute piece of criticism which reveals once more the element of symmetry in the poem), we object, Not so! Nature-as-Destiny has given him the character which under the influence of the stars here conflicts with other destinal powers. I shall not go on listing instances where critical insight is based on the assumption that Chaucer's characters have free will, but the evidence is sufficiently abundant, and on any other terms, of course, the characters represent nothing more than fate fighting with itself.

Must we give up the full meaning of Criseyde's character, that of a clear-headed young woman who looks the facts calmly in the face until she learns the necessity of self-deceit? Shall we say that her paradox is only that produced by destiny, and that her candor is only an entirely meaningless reverie in which a human being is under the illusion that she is deciding her future course of action (whereas she is passive and impotent, while forces work and stimuli produce their quota of reaction)? No blame attaches to anybody in this

scheme, not even to Calchas, time-server that he is, but
fortunate indeed on this plan; for all are moved simply by
the wind, the weather, and the rain. And if modern criticism
has generally proceeded on a false basis, allowing some degree of responsibility to the characters, Geoffrey Chaucer has
been just as guilty, and at least part of the time has been
under the same illusion; for in the *Legend of Good Women* he
refers with apparent sincerity to the sin of Criseyde, and even
in the *Troilus* acknowledges her "gilt," when it would have
been a matter of the greatest simplicity, in the very passage
in which he writes her defense, to say that she was really the
victim of circumstance. He would, he says, excuse her for
very pity. Why then, at this point, does he fail even so much
as to mention fate and stars? But it is clear that we have no
right to trust Chaucer's honesty, if he is really a determinist;
for in the Epilogue he speaks of the pagans' cursed ancient
ways and lauds Christian ethic (although on this basis we
know from the passion in the earlier lines that he secretly
prefers the warm sensuality of the story which contradicts it). The Epilogue, in fact, he added only as a sop
to the pious, and then (as we are fairly certain that he
inserted the soliloquy of Troilus still later) he went back
to deepen the pagan element (which, according to some
critics, was really opposed to his own philosophy). Surely
this is a new Chaucer, and one that we have never met
hitherto.

Is this really the upshot of the story? If so, why not leave
the matter at the meagre summary given in the opening lines
of the poem? The author's purpose is merely to tell of
Troilus

In lovynge, how his aventures fellen
Fro wo to wele, and after out of joie. . . .
                                        i, 3–4.

Do we conceive of Chaucer writing the long and admittedly
beautiful Epilogue to keep the orthodox undisturbed, and
then returning to the poem to intensify elements out of harmony with it? Is most of the criticism up to date based on
illusions in the critics no less than on those in the characters,
especially when that criticism finds a richer meaning in the
poem from the very fact of its implications of free will? All
this is no exaggeration of our problem. If anyone uses determinism to imply merely an emphasis on the occasional
futility (and not the unreality) of human will power in gain-
ing material ends, then let us have that clearly stated; but
such a view is in accordance with orthodox medieval philosophy (as the whole tradition of Fortune and Fate shows),
and even that interpretation is not wholly fair to the action
of the piece. Chaucer, and for some centuries his readers as
well, have been concerned with the degree of blame to
attach to Criseyde, who is often cited as guilty of the cardinal
sin of faithlessness. It is absurd to compare the poem with
tragedies like *Macbeth* and *Othello* and *Lear*, but in all these
cases the touch of human frailty explains what follows, and
greater consequences follow the "dram of eale" than the
characters can foresee.

But the *Troilus* is not to be taken on such a scale. It is a
poem of youth. Its high seriousness is in part that of youth,
and its suffering really ends with Troilus's grief over losing
Criseyde. The death of the hero, as Chaucer makes quite
clear, is not an immediate part of the tragic sequence. It is

caused in an affair entirely outside of his connection with the story of Criseyde (v, 1763–1764, and 1806. Cf. *Filos.* viii, st. 26–27). His death must come sometime and it comes in this way to release his spirit for the flight that permits him to scan his own career and see its meaning. His flight to a Christian heaven is no stranger than the original flight of Scipio Africanus or the later one of Pompey the Great to what is substantially the same heaven. Dante shows us the Trojan Ripheus in Paradise, and we understand the point. Again Chaucer took great pains in composing the passage; and in this celestial region we as critics, like Troilus, may learn a sense of proportion. Among other things we may learn to understand that the sin of Troilus was not grave or mortal, nor his tragedy of stupendous and lasting significance (we do not observe that, as a sop to the pious, Troilus was plunged into hell), and that the apparatus of the Court of Love is mere tinkling symbolism as the strife of the critics is often sounding brass. The Epilogue no more contradicts the mood of the poem than various tendencies of human nature in one person contradict one another; on any other terms every Christian would have to be a complete ascetic and every Catholic a puritan. It is an aspect of Chaucer's greatness and his breadth that he can enter as heartily into the love affair as into the vision of the limitation of earthly things and the supreme value of lasting idealism.

4

Surely it is a safe principle in criticizing a great work of art to assume that the interpretation in harmony with all parts of the poem is the one nearest to the intention of the author.

Another good principle to assume is that a great artist knows what he is about, and that he has a right to be understood on his own terms. In all fairness, in the interpretation of the *Troilus*, how can we reject the Epilogue and deny any Christian meaning in the passages on Fortune? Can we throw overboard all criticism up to now because of a recrudescent psychological fad? Shall we hold that Chaucer intended one meaning for the Christians of his day and another, assuming that they were a different group, for those who liked a kind of pagan tragedy, the very existence of which is doubtful in that period? And, finally, can we assume that, for the sake of the thrill, the poet used an alien philosophy to get his effects?

This last point is one that deserves a moment's special attention. Has Chaucer used determinism for artistic purposes in the body of the poem, and then added the Epilogue as a later *confessio fidei* to set the public at rest about himself? This is a wholly different matter from Milton's using a geocentric system of astronomy for *Paradise Lost*, or from Wordsworth's calling on Platonism for the poetic truth of the *Ode on Intimations of Immortality*. Determinism implies a special attitude toward life as a whole. It is, I believe, an unworthy conception of the nature of art to hold that a writer may adopt for the nonce whatever philosophy has artistic value and play it for its effect as if it meant nothing in particular. Before we commit ourselves to such a theory we must see important examples of the trick furnished by great writers, examples generally accepted as such by competent critics. A recent attempt to demonstrate that such is the case with Shakespeare is a palpable failure. To play with philosophy for the sake of a sensation is hardly characteristic of any poet who sees art as a source of something more than ordinary pleasure.

If we accept Chaucer's terms the poem is in harmony with his philosophy. Troilus on earth may expound determinism with all the determination of his desperate nature; but from the heights of heaven, looking back with more humor, he abandons the idea and admits his folly. There are thus two layers of meaning in the poem, symmetrically adjusted, as we have seen, to each other: Troilus was guilty of sinning against the Court of Love, and was punished by Criseyde's infidelity; from the Christian point of view, he was guilty of yielding to blind pleasure, and he suffered. Doubly therefore he was responsible for what occurred. The dedication to Gower and Strode, which causes difficulty for those who take another view, is thus explained as delightfully appropriate. The poet, not too gravely and not without impudence, agrees with these gentlemen for at least once. It has been remarked earlier in this study that the poem may seem almost like the presentation of a particular case of the workings of chance, with the *Consolation of Philosophy* as a background. The caprice of Fortune exalts and lowers the unhappy Troilus; the question of free will is raised, and the process is roughly similar to that of the *Consolatio* up to the solution. Here again we may observe that the solution in the poem is precisely that furnished by Boethius, who also bids men to lift their eyes to the contemplation of eternal values; Troilus in fact proceeds to eternity where all these difficulties are made plain. The conclusion of Boethius, although suggesting no verbal influence, represents in sum the moral of the Epilogue:

"... and God, byholdere and forwytere of alle thingis, duelleth above, and the present eternite of his sighte renneth alwey with the diverse qualite of our dedes, dispensynge and ordeynynge medes to gode men and tormentz to wikkide men. Ne in ydel ne in veyn ne ben ther put in God hope and preyeris, that ne mowen nat ben unspedful ne withouten effect whan they been ryghtful.

"Withstond thanne and eschue thou vices; worschipe and love thou vertues; areise thi corage to ryghtful hopes; yilde thou humble preieres an heygh. Gret necessite of prowesse and vertu is encharged and comaunded to yow, yif ye nil nat dissimulen; syn that ye worken and don ... byforn the eyen of the Iuge that seeth and demeth alle thinges."

V, pr. vi, 328 ff.

The spirit of the *Consolatio* is in the *Troilus*, its hymns are taken over in various parts of the poem, its philosophy quoted here and there, and the final moral is the same. To urge that in the *Troilus* the feeling of the sections regarding love and passion is really pagan, and therefore totally opposed to the mood of the Epilogue, is like objecting to the sympathetic presentation of the grief of Boethius in the *Consolatio* when the moral enlightenment bestowed by Philosophy is later to follow. In the Epilogue the influence of Boethius on Chaucer's own conception of life in its more important aspects is finally complete.

Elsewhere Chaucer again studies the problem of fate. Chauntecleer in the *Nun's Priest's Tale* is fearful of what destiny has in store for him, his wife causes him much trouble, and his tragedy is linked with that of Troy and Rome as well (B. 4545 ff.). One might take the following lines as indicative of Chaucer's settled determinism:

> O destinee, that mayst nat been eschewed!
> Alas, that Chauntecleer fleigh fro the bemes!

> Allas, his wyf ne roghte nat of dremes!
> And on a Friday fil al this meschaunce.
>
> B. 4528 ff.

But the fates seem to be in conflict once more, Fortune steps in to help the hero, and apparently if a man keeps his eyes open he can take advantage of celestial indecision.

> "For he that wynketh, whan he sholde see,
> Al wilfully, God lat him nevere thee!"
>
> B. 4621-4622.

Haec fabula docet. Chaucer's head was where it should be, and he did not cultivate a sentimental art at the expense of common sense.

Chapter V

THE LEGEND OF GOOD WOMEN

WHAT can be said for the *Legend of Good Women*? Despite the grace and freshness of the Prologue, which may be enjoyed in either of its two forms although B is more spontaneous and A is better ordered, the work as a whole is usually found dull. The somber note of the martyrdom of the fair ladies is one that admits of little variation. The poem should be studied, I believe, against the background of the whole controversy about women which came to the surface from time to time in the Middle Ages and greatly occupied the attention of some important writers, among whom was certainly Chaucer. He had translated at least part of the *Roman de la Rose*, a poem that was really notorious for Jean de Meun's unflattering portrayal of feminine temperament; in the *Troilus* he had described a heroine who was guilty, however charmingly, of the worst of sins. If, as Lydgate tells us, the *Legend* was written at the request of the queen, and if it shows signs of being an ingenious response to an invitation of this kind, nevertheless Chaucer did not stop there with his discussion of the woman question. The topic comes up again in a far more significant way. It is the seed that flowers in the most magnificent creation he ever achieved: the character of the Wife of Bath and the drama of the Marriage Cycle.

It is not surprising in any age to find that the problem of

woman is what chiefly occupies a poet's imagination. In the Middle Ages this was sure to be the case in many instances because — whether poets usually hymn of love or not — the social status of the fair sex was a matter of argument on every side. The heritage of dignity ascribed to women by the culture that preceded medievalism was not impressive. According to Islam the female has no soul until she marries. The Roman lady certainly won more respect than that; but Tacitus seems prompted to castigate conditions among his own people when he presents a very favorable view of the way the Germans regarded their women. According to him the Germans thought of them as prophetesses, even as divine. Doubtless the goddesses, in the Germanic as also in the Celtic mythology, reflected the reverence for the inescapably noble attributes of women of which men could hardly be unaware. But one has only to read Bede's account of St Hilda to see what an advance is made with the coming of Christianity to the western world. Judaism had known of the prudent woman whose industry lends honor to her family, and whose children learn to call her blessed (*Prov.* xxxi); but this is a whole world different from the revelation that came with the Virgin Mary. Where once a place in the ancient temple had been set apart for women, that men might not be contaminated, now the great gift of the Incarnation was through a woman, worthy beyond all other creatures. Such a fact could not fail to modify the European attitude toward daughters, sisters, and wives as well as mothers.

The cult of the Virgin was not, as many seem to suppose, an invention of the twelfth or perhaps even the thirteenth century. She was called the "Mother of God" at least as early as the Council of Ephesus (431); by the seventh century a string of churches across Europe were dedicated to her and named in her honor. She appears depicted in the Catacombs as early as the second century, and by the sixth she appears in mosaics. Her assumption is shown in an eighth-century linen at Sens, and in a ninth- or tenth-century ivory at St Gall. The *Ave* was recited in Old English. In addition to these few facts many more might be cited to show the veneration offered to her throughout the Middle Ages beginning with the earliest years; and the point is that men could not have fallen on their knees to invoke her prayers, or those of any other of the women saints, without an appreciable effect on their attitude toward women in general. The teaching of St Paul that wives should be subject to their husbands, the preaching of the monks that the weakness of Eve still threatened mankind, could not modify the view that women have after all a celestial importance.

On the worldly side too in the literature of love the idea grew that women could inspire and exalt men to a vision of nobler living. Ironically enough someone has suggested that this theory may have developed from Moslem sources, but it reached Christian writers and filled the poems of the troubadours and the authors of the *dolce styl nuovo* until it found supreme expression in Dante's *Divine Comedy*. When centuries later Goethe speaks of the eternal feminine leading us upward and onward, he says what would have been inconceivable before the Middle Ages. Whether the poetry of this school gave its phrases to the literature of devotion to Our Lady, or whether (as is doubtful) the influence went the other way, does not much matter; the religious devotion combined with the secular to raise a proper respect for women. And this fact is obvious in the great controversy on the subject that flourished for centuries in the latter part of the period. For not every one was pleased when a pedestal was first offered to woman, whether saint or feudal mistress. Treatises were written, poems composed, invectives and diatribes launched, to the effect that women were frail and fickle. Of these the most noteworthy was Jean de Meun's part of the *Roman de la Rose*, which borrowed its disillusion from realistic passages in Ovid, and described woman as hypocritical, vain, dishonest, and scheming. A lady, says Jean through the words of the Duenna, cannot keep to one suitor. She must have several. I use the translation, with some changes, of Mr. F. S. Ellis:

> And so a damsel fair ywis
> When mistress of the field she is,
> And may at will her suitors please,
> Good right hath she their gold to seize, —
> Nay, she would be a fool indeed
> Who failed her interest to speed
> Through giving all her love to one.

Only recall, says he, the sad cases of Dido, Phyllis, Oenone, Medea, and the rest, who suffered from being constant to one man. Furthermore, a lady must see to it that by the use of paint and powder she is as beautiful as she can be.

> Women should learn to cry with grace,
> But they so oft find time and place
> For tears, I need not teach them how
> To weep — they know that well, I vow.

> For every woman in her eye
> Stores tears, and one and all can cry
> At will. . . .

He goes on to set forth the tricks of these artful creatures. The lady's costume must be suited to her loveliness, and she must know how to manage it:

> Or as she knows right well to do,
> She just uplifts her gown a few
> Short inches, quicker pace to suit,
> Disclosing thus her winsome foot,
> With hope that all the passers by
> Its dainty form and turn may spy.

In making love she must be artful:

> As he more vehement doth grow
> More hesitation should she show.

At last when yielding she must protest:

> I yield to you for love alone,
> Through presents you had never won
> My virgin heart. . . .
> Ah! wicked man, who knew the style
> That would my maiden's soul beguile.

When she has him, she must rob the poor man of everything he has:

> The more that women make men pay,
> The more, far more, beloved are they.
>
> .   .   .   .   .   .
>
> To fleece a gull may many aid:
> Her valets and her chambermaid,
> Her sister, nurse, and many another,
> And e'en with equal zest, her mother. . . .

And finally, after taking from the wretch all he owns, the lady must throw him over by pretending to be enraged at some unknown perfidy of his. So ends the fine story. Jean de Meun adds the observation that, though women are enslaved by law, Nature has made them achieve freedom. Birds in a cage flutter against the bars:

> And every woman doth possess
> Within her that same restlessness.

Except in Criseyde's speech of surrender, Chaucer's heroine in the *Troilus* is nothing like the creature here displayed. We see here instead something more like a picture of the Wife of Bath in her youth. But I anticipate. People learned passages from the *Roman de la Rose* by heart just as to-day they know lines from *Hamlet* or *The Merchant of Venice*. Everyone knew the poem. And to-day one can drive to the little town of Meung-sur-Loire where Jean lived, and see a statue put up in his honor. It displays a lovely lady offering him a rose. It must have been carved by someone who hadn't read his poem. Certainly no woman who had read it would have offered him a tribute of this kind.

In the early part of the fourteenth century Guillaume de Guileville wrote his three huge allegories about the pilgrimage of man in the heavens above as well as in the earth beneath, in size out-topping Bunyan's work and almost Dante's. Here in a long passage Guillaume attempted to rebuke Jean de Meun, and implied that his doctrines were an assault on the principle of chastity. John Lydgate, monk of Bury St Edmunds, translated the allegory which contained these lines. In France another attack on women was launched in the *Lamentationes Matheoli*, written in the thirteenth cen-

tury and translated into French in the fourteenth. Related
material was incorporated in the treatise of the "Goodman of
Paris," who wrote to prepare his wife, much younger than
he, for her probable second adventure into matrimony. And
at about the same time there was living in Paris the lovely
Christine de Pisan, who was a militant feminist if ever there
was one. In 1399 she wrote her *Epistre au Dieu d'Amours*, in
which Cupid comes to woman's aid and attacks Jean de
Meun's *Roman*:

> How long the tale! what tangles have we here!
> Mixture of science gloomy, dark, and drear,
> Adventures too and wiles of every kind
> Just to deceive a simple maiden's mind. . . .

A fairly just estimate I should say! Cupid recalls the great instances of faithful and distinguished ladies, and even exoner-
ates poor Eve of having deceived Adam. Christine's poem
was translated into fifteenth-century English by Thomas
Hoccleve, who was moved again to write in women's behalf, explaining, among other things, that although originally woman was made from a rib she is not therefore
crooked: the rib is circular and a circle is the perfect figure
in geometry. A number of other works in English on the
great problem of woman's estate might be cited. But in
France Christine stirred up a tempest. The details are well
known. Before she got through, she involved in her controversy the Prévost of the city of Lille, the secretary of
Charles VI, the chancellor of the University of Paris (the
great Gerson), and even the Queen of France herself. Unmoved by all this Christine went serenely on, disposing of
Jean de Meun and her enemies too, proposing an educational

program for women, and inviting them to intelligence and also to a proper humility. She does not ask them to compete with man or to deprive him of his position of honor in the world.

At the end then of a great debate lasting about two hundred years the rights of woman were vindicated, if gently, and Christine managed her part of the warfare with dignity and charm. We may see her to-day in a manuscript illumination. Her face looks sensitive and rather elfish. As she writes she appears to be amused by the close attention of the little white dog at her feet. All in all she was a most interesting lady, and comes out of the battle with rather better grace, I think, than the eighteenth-century Mary Wollstonecraft, who wrote on the independence of woman but pursued a man across Europe. The business of getting a fair recognition for women has been a long and tedious process. Let us remember how much the Middle Ages contributed to all this. It is part of the history of Christianity, an influence of the cult of the Virgin Mary, a development springing from poetry and the troubadours and medieval allegory, and notably the result in part of the efforts of a delightful lady in France named Christine de Pisan.

Against all this background how does Chaucer's contribution appear? In general it shows him in his usual attitude on questions of reform. He does not seem to care much, at least on the surface. He is not lecturing anybody as a rule, and the temper of his verse is totally different from that of the *Vision of Piers Plowman* or even from that of "moral Gower." Presumably Queen Anne asked him to do penance for his heresy against love in his translation of the *Roman de la Rose* and in the *Troilus*. Perhaps she even dictated the nature of the exercise he was to write. In any case he responded with the *Legend*, which in tracery and style is more like a valentine in certain respects than the more heavily weighted *Parliament of Fowls*. It certainly is not a serious or even a half-serious defence of woman, such as Christine might have chosen to write. It reveals in fact a delicately comic element which I think has been missed by those readers who have enjoyed its frail charm. Of course the humor of transferring religious conventions to the poetry of love has been long understood; the idea of Cupid's saints, parallel to the saints of the Church, continues the sort of appeal to mild mirth familiar in many instances elsewhere. Medieval people knew all about the commandments of love, the lover's confessional, the liturgy of the worship of Venus, so that such devices were worn a little pale by Chaucer's day.

But with all due allowance for the point that the *Legend* has to do with matters of love and fidelity, the fact that Cleopatra leads off the list — "Cleopatre with al thy passioun" — is, I still think, impressive. At the very least it accents the difference in the setting as a collection of love's legends, and thus the poet has intensified the value of this form of transfer of conventions. The result is something close to impudence. So too is the parallel, recently noted by a sharp critic, of the Queen of Love to the Virgin Mary and of the God of Love to the person of Christ. And I also think that the passage at the beginning about the need of authority where experience is lacking shows a similar echo of the ecclesiastical. The implication here follows that faithful woman are not often found in real life. To read such meaning into the context has been called absurd, on the ground that such an insinuation would be cowardly; but that objection is valid only if we exaggerate the import of the discussion. At worst it is only an appeal for proof of good women (according to the standards of Courtly Love) in real life; it is in the mood of banter, and is in no worse taste than countless jokes exchanged in the world's history on the theme of woman's frailty. As for the Queen the poem seems to imply that she is in part at least, in a kind of hovering allusiveness, symbolized in Alceste, whose virtues reflect hers and who among faithful wives takes leading place.

Since this interpretation may be disputed, I may pause for a moment to follow Chaucer's procedure more in detail. The poem refers at the very start to the thousand times he has heard of the joy of heaven and the pain of hell, and then goes on at length to discuss the fact that nevertheless one has to take all this on authority. So one turns to books, he says, for authority in regard to doctrine, and to get stories of holiness, of hate, and so on.

> Wel ought us thanne honouren and beleve
> These bokes, there we han noon other preve.
>
> F. 27–28.

The idea is retained in G. 27–28, rendered more precise by revision:

> Wel oughte us thanne on olde bokes leve,
> Ther as there is non other assay by preve.

Now an experienced poet, certainly a genius, does not begin an extensive work like the *Legend* without some design; the opening passage of his composition will hardly be a matter of chance. Of course all this introduction is part of the quasi-ecclesiastical tone of the poem, and in that guise, does very well. But what is it that we are asked to take on authority in this emphatic manner? He continues with his discussion to say that he himself delights to read books and gives them his faith and credence. Then he narrates his own adventure of going to see the daisy (and in F. tells of the honor he pays to his lady). In the revised form of the Prologue (G.), changing the original a little, he wrote:

> But wherfore that I spak, to yeve credence
> To bokes olde and don hem reverence,
> Is for men shulde autoritees beleve,
> There as ther lyth non other assay by preve.
> For myn entente is, or I fro yow fare,
> The naked text in English to declare
> Of many a story, or elles of many a geste,
> As autours seyn; leveth hem if yow leste!
>
> G. 81–88.

Then he sees (in a dream in both versions) the procession of the God of Love, who reproaches him for telling so many stories against women. Could he not find in his memory or in his books (according to G.) some story of women that were good and true? The books he has — Valerye, Titus, and the rest — have they nothing in them about clean maidens, true wives, steadfast widows, and especially about "trouthe" and the woe they endure for fidelity? Later Love says (in G. 528) that the poet knows the goodness of women by "pref" as well as "by storyes herebyforn," and he points the remark with immediate reference to Alceste. This I suppose to be a tactful compliment to the Queen. He never lets the problem of authorities quite drop from his attention. Plainly the implication is that Chaucer is to search books for evidence about faithful and good women.

A lady listening to such a discourse would be prompted to ask at once why the poet did not look for some examples among his acquaintances. Surely the Prologue is tactless, she would insist. If the beginning means anything, it implies that in default of instances in real life the author must turn to authorities. The suggestion, however slight, is there, quite definitely put in the initial reference to the unknowable facts about Heaven and Hell which he takes on faith. Later of Cleopatra he says the tale is "storyal soth, it is no fable" (702). Thisbe at her death exclaims: may God forbid a woman cannot be as true in loving as a man! And as the stories proceed the poet apparently finds in his books the moral that while women are faithful, men may not be trusted (1254 ff.; 2387):

> Be war, ye wemen, of youre subtyl fo,
> Syn yit this day men may ensaumple se;
> And trusteth, as in love, no man but me.
>
> 2559–2561.

So the authorities justify women for the most part, and there are examples in real life if one look for them. But does such a conclusion stultify the original insinuation? Is it cowardly of the poet to propose an accusation in which he really does not believe? Such inferences demand a logic which the tone of the discourse does not in the least suggest, and lay an impossible burden on the lightness of touch which the poet clearly means to sustain. In a sense the logic is not violated anyhow: the poet, it would seem, is under the charge of being skeptical regarding the faithfulness of women and has to turn to the authorities; in the passage recently quoted the "ensaumple" to be seen in life is the faithless man, but that does not in itself prove the fidelity of his *amie*.

But I pause for a moment of wonder why none of the plots in the great stories, like those of Dido and Cleopatra, sufficiently set Chaucer's imagination going to win for us a more significant work of art. Here in the sufferings of these ladies was potential drama. Where is the dialogue, where are the touch and go, of sparkling realism and sense of human interplay, where is the genuine note of tragedy however lightly sounded like that which the poet had given to the world in his *Troilus*? Here in the *Legend* what he chiefly cares for is "routhe," and that, it seems, as a matter of duty. Perhaps he felt that in dealing with these martyred heroines, humor was not fitting; that humor somehow cancels pity. Yet such is not his customary manner, even in other equally delicate situations like that in the *Book of the Duchess*. Now and then, to be sure, we do perceive his smile, as when of Pyramus he writes:

> Upon that o syde of the wal stod he,
> And on that other side stod Thesbe.
>
> 750-751.

But in general his solemnity is like that which appears in the *Man of Law's Tale* and the *Physician's Tale*; in fact it has been suggested that these stories were once meant for the *Legend*, although manifestly in theme they do not follow the problem of fidelity. Perhaps it was because virtuous women in distress did not seem to him especially funny. I shall

have something to say again about his treatment of pity;
but here I must admit, I cannot think that these narratives
are thin simply because his emotions were taken up with the
afflicted virtue of Cleopatra or Dido. He may have thought
that his audience must be stirred; but why, we wonder, did
his imagination fail to leap to his task when he began to
write of such a scene as that where Aeneas leaves Dido? Even
if like Trollope he wrote his stint every day, why did such
an opportunity fail to quicken his thought and enrich the
ink of his pen?

I am led to reflect on the sort of plots where Chaucer's
creative powers were actually fired and where his production wants no trace of vitality. The *Troilus*, of course, shows
full power, but there he had the *Filostrato* already passion-
ately alive to stir him; and it is certain that its inspiration
lasted beyond the composition of his own poem. The *Prioress's Tale?* yes, the poignancy of childhood moved him as it
did in the address of Constance to her child; but pathos alone
did not get him very far in the *Monk's Tale* or in the story
of St Cecilia. Pathos is not the only moving factor in the
story of Griselda; and here the poet added lines showing a
touch of rebelliousness in the heroine, and he later gave the
tale a setting that threw a humorous light on certain features.
Pathos can hardly be said to evoke his fullest artistic response;
only compare how richly it inspired Dickens. Some of
Chaucer's pathetic narratives were perhaps written by request, but they are not his best work. Humor and irony
draw his interest without doubt, as one can see in the *Tale
of Sir Thopas* and in the swift effectiveness of the story of the
rioters. But the Prologue of the *Wife of Bath's Tale*, with all

its implications and echoes in the Marriage Cycle, is where the poet most surely reveals that his powers were functioning at their wealthiest; and here he began (as in fact with the *Troilus*) by dealing with his material in terms — not merely of humor or plot but — of character. The same is true of the Canterbury pilgrimage. The Wife of Bath came into being, I suppose, when he was reading about traits of female character in Deschamps's *Miroir de Mariage*, or possibly when he was contemplating some lurid women he had known, rich in human traits. So too with the other pilgrims; the abundance of his genius finds expression in terms of character, and, however much humor and pathos come into play, fundamentally it is human character that starts him at his best. He may begin his narrative with other things, as in the *House of Fame* or the *Parliament*, but sooner or later he gravitates toward character and its concerns. The reason then, I think, that Chaucer did not make much of the story of Cleopatra or Phyllis and the rest is that he began, not with character, but with a proposition.

I am afraid it was beginning with the moral that injured the *Legend*. M. Cazamian thinks the poem was left unfinished because "its subject and a humorous disposition agree too ill together." But the full humorous purpose the poet must have pretty well forgotten after composing the Prologue. No, it was the moral that lent thinness to the stories, and finally destroyed the whole plan. It was too simple, like virtue unalloyed, useful perhaps in allegories but less stimulating to the imagination of an artist. Whether Chaucer liked the moral, however, has little to do with the case; the point is that he thought of his plots with reference to that rather than to the creatures he was presenting. Characterization, however good, is not brought to the fore in the sources he used: he relied on the *Roman d'Enéas* rather more than the *Aeneid*, and on Ovid and the *Ovide Moralizé*. He was led to think of the plot first and how that illustrated his theme. If he had begun to write of the Canterbury pilgrims with strict reference to sins and virtues, I believe he would have collapsed along the way. Even in a fable like the *Nun's Priest's Tale* what he cares about is Chantecler and Pertelote; one suspects he thought of them at times entirely without considering the moral, and the marvelous dialogue on dreams has little justification in the lesson at the end. All this is only what has happened before. Like a good writer in any age he did his best when he began with character and worked out his plot accordingly; but beyond most writers the thought of character filled and fructified his imagination to an extraordinary degree. It is certain that he loved people. That in the *Legend* he was a little irked by the business of having a set moral may appear in the slightly flippant treatment in the Prologue of the theme of faithful wives.

On the other hand, one of the good things in the *Legend* is the poet's little joke about his being an enemy to love. I wonder who originated that. Perhaps a lady at Court — I will not suggest the Queen herself; perhaps it was only the poet, bent on getting some idea for the poem which must be written. The idea that he had poor success in such matters he had presented before. Here one thinks of the Queen setting his task for him, and we can imagine how he took it. Another Queen enjoined upon Shakespeare the task of showing Falstaff in love. Here again a compliment of a sort was attempted: the invincible hero who defeated Dame Quickly was for once to find his match, to be discomfited and, of all things, by the ladies. But it would not work. Here again the poet began with a proposition instead of with the character he already knew; the upshot is that the new hero is not Falstaff, and the play is not on the level of the Falstaff scenes in *Henry the Fourth*.

Yet there may be just a hard grain of truth in the accusation that Chaucer was an enemy to love, that is, if we mean love *paramours*. Readers have long suspected that in each case his poems of Courtly Love were meant to celebrate devotion, not of the secret lover for his *amie* but, within the bonds of matrimony, of perfectly domestic attachments. Certainly the *Book of the Duchess* mourns the death of John of Gaunt's beloved wife; in all probability the *House of Fame* and the *Parliament of Fowls* presented tidings of a betrothal for which congratulation was due. Loving wifehood is the special merit of Alceste in the *Legend*. According to the *Troilus* amorous preoccupations of a worldly sort carry their own peril and are not ultimately satisfying. In all this the poet is hardly puritanical or heavily moral; but to some of his friends, at least, he must have seemed the victim of certain frustrating convictions. In their eyes, his *joie de vivre* carried him only so far, indeed had an element of pretence in it. The man could tell lively stories with the best of them and yet in his private life he was after all pretty much the hermit. Possibly here is the reason for his frequent declaration that he is unsuccessful in love: he has had an eight years' love-sickness, he says, but gets nowhere; like Pandarus in the dance of love he "hops always behind." But why protest so much? Well, it may have been a kind of protection for a man who did not go in for that sort of thing.

But there is another and equally plausible interpretation of his attitude, and it may as well be fairly considered. Such protests are not likely to come from a man who is really unsuccessful in love. It is silly to suppose that they are a reflection of marital unhappiness or a troublesome wife or anything like that. To be sure, shrewish wives are several times shown in the *Canterbury Tales* and their links, but so are constant and patient and submissive and devoted wives. If there was trouble in the poet's own *ménage* (caused, say, by a Flemish father-in-law "dit Paonnet" — "called *peacock*" or "*pawn*" — and Chaucer's making fun of the Flemish Sir Thopas), I doubt if he talked about it or made allusions to it in his verse; I doubt if it was likely to stir the spirit of fun even in his robust nature if the trouble had any gravity. If he was sensible he probably would not care to satirize his wife even by veiled allusion. On the other hand, if from time to time he attempted some other love affair and met with rejection, he would hardly proclaim it even as a joke in his verse. These things are obvious, but they seem to be occasionally forgotten by commentators. The cast-off suitor does not boast about his failure. Pandarus, it is true, openly bewails his lack of advance in such matters, and Troilus implies (I, 622) that his friend has repeatedly failed. Yet on this very point, I would suggest, Pandarus is not a wholly admirable figure; his weakness on this score fits in with his passionate zeal for helping the hero, and here, I think, is the trait that in an extremely indirect way furnishes the chief development in his character when Shakespeare takes him over. M. Legouis was not accurate in his observation that Chaucer's Pandarus makes us see double; makes us aware, that is, of the figure in the *Filostrato* and of that in Shakespeare's play. The change in the later drama rests on the expansion of one side of Pandarus's character, and it drops most of his charm and all his freshness. The result is, not more of the same person we have had before but, a different kind of person. Except for name and function, in other words, Chaucer's intermediary would not make us think of Shakespeare's. The dramatist's character does not jest about his failures in love; he has not the almost creative delight in his task we find in Chaucer's figure, but rather a disgusted persistence. In the first point he was potentially more attractive; but when I speak of a trait that Shakespeare did develop in his revision of the story, I mean that something of the futility of Chaucer's Pandarus is carried over into the corresponding character's attitude toward his unsavory business in the play.

In general isn't it the strong and not the weak, the privately well rewarded and not the frustrated, who may pretend to have no luck in love? This is the way to kiss and not tell. One thinks of the counterpart of this in the group described in the *House of Fame* who wanted great renown for achievements:

> "As wel of love as other thyng.
> Al was us never broche ne ryng,
> Ne elles noght, from wymmen sent,
> Ne ones in her herte yment

> To make us oonly frendly chere,
> But myghten temen us upon bere;
> Yet lat us to the peple seme
> Suche as the world may of us deme
> That wommen loven us for wod."
>
> 1739–1747.

Pandarus in his talk with Troilus on the subject of the "avauntour" in love expresses something of the same idea (iii, 302 ff.):

> "And for the more part, al is untrewe
> That men of yelpe, and it were brought to preve."
>
> *Troilus*, iii, 306–307.

The upshot of all this discussion is that if these disclaimers on Chaucer's part indicate anything, they may well indicate that in love affairs he had his own private career. But of course they are rather conventional Court of Love poetry, and no inference of the sort can really be drawn.

Yet why does he adopt such a silly convention at all? I revert to my original suggestion. Isn't it probable that this was the pose Chaucer regularly sustained in such matters among his friends? — he did not cultivate episodes of love; the natural response in jest at Court would be that he was an enemy to love; he was no preacher, and the easiest way out was to say that he had no luck. Perhaps, like the family joke Cressid turns on Pandarus, the idea furnished sport for certain ladies of elegance, accusing the poet much as the God of Love does in the *Legend*. And he was ready for them, and took up the theme on their own terms, and gave them as good as he got. The *Legend of Good Women* is at least as effective as that, with its banter about authority and the need of searching books for what is not found in life, and finally with its real compliment that women are less faithless than men.

I am puzzled, however, by the absence of another very important feature in the *Legend*. Aside from the Prologue why did so little poetry get into it? Why did the poet's imagination fail to waken at the opportunities in such an idea as that of the metamorphosis of Philomena? Perhaps it was the hours Chaucer set himself for writing, or perhaps it was his methodical purpose. The Prologue itself is fresh, but even there the poetry is often taken over in businesslike fashion from others, Deschamps or Froissart or another source. The fact that he chose the poetic material was partly conditioned by his plan; the freshness of spirit in the lines derived, it may be, from the poet's original zest for the opening part. The high point of his inspiration poetically was when the music of the ladies' names led him to compose the Balade, and he may have written that long before the Prologue. Here is music; but here he was not occupied with the stories of the heroines told patiently one after another to prove a point. It is odd that when he got to the stories themselves none of these famous creatures captivated him, although he had sung of them sweetly enough; not Cleopatra, not Lucrece, none of them could lure him to break over the traces of his scheme. When one stops to think of it, isn't it surprising that in the *Troilus* when he came to describe great Helen of Troy, his imagination apparently was not sent racing, as — to take an example from another realm — Swinburne's was with Guinivere in his *Tristram of Lyonesse* even at the expense, for the moment, of Iseult? Yet Chaucer's Helen is a gracious figure, and more about her part in the story would perhaps have injured the proportion of the episode.

Possibly at the time of composing the *Legend* he still remembered Criseyde and was under her spell. There seems to be little doubt that he loved her, and he may have continued to fear her treachery in every beautiful woman. Artistically at least he had had a vivid experience of Cressid's faithlessness, and so henceforth for him faithful women existed only in books and their stories were legendary. This conception may be more than fanciful. Throughout his life his most realistic portraits of women show the faithless type. But this is not to say that here in the *Legend* he gives us only personified abstractions; even in his allegories Doux Penser, Daunger, Idleness, and others of the kind do not crowd his canvas, and in moving from his earlier work to his later there is no sudden jump from symbolism to real characterization. One may suspect that he neglected Dido, Cleopatra, and the rest, because his work did not begin with a consideration of what they were really like. With the exception of Alisoun in the *Miller's Tale* and of course Criseyde, he seems to notice character even before the loveliness of women. Here, I think, is something like proof that the poet did not go in for successive love affairs. Charm of course wins him but that is because it is an expression of personality; and his great ladies, Blanche the Duchess, Criseyde, the Prioress, the Wife of Bath, all have charm in abundance, but they also have distinct and rich personalities.

What then is Chaucer's contribution to the long dispute about women that furnished a theme for so many medieval writers? His ostensible offering to this literature is light-hearted to a degree, not to say flippant. He will defend ladies, yes, but his argument is rather artificial. His mood is a bit ironic, and his work hardly absorbed his best energies. Yet one cannot say that the *Legend* represents all he had in mind on the subject. In the *Canterbury Tales* there are ladies of distinction richly and sympathetically described. He does not present the sex as faultless; he sees both good and bad. But his writing on this theme is like that which he offers on other questions; he is immensely taken with human beings, he finds them abundantly worthy of respect and liking. Women such as he presents, whether it be the distressed Constance, or wily Alisoun, or submissive Griselda, or May or Dorigen, are never soulless, never mere chattels; they are always tremendously important. For it is a curious thing that while Chaucer exposes human weakness, at that very instant he establishes human dignity. If his characters show that they have fallen, they have fallen from a level of some importance. His women are, it is true, chiefly engaged with thoughts about men, even the ladies who in the *Troilus* are found reading the romance of Thebes. But they are more than subjects merely of entertainment; and Constance, Virginia, Prudence, Griselda, and the Prioress, are meant to elicit admiration. His treatment of the problem of woman's freedom in the Wife of Bath's prologue is again ironic; but the essential question, that of *maistrye*, is really considered with due seriousness underlying the comedy of the Marriage Cycle, and the conclusion as presented in the *Franklin's Tale* shows a full understanding of woman's rights. Chaucer, intentionally or not, echoes in fact the *Roman de la Rose* as he settles the matter:

Love wol nat been constreyned by maistrye.
Whan maistrie comth, the God of Love anon
Beteth his wynges, and farewel, he is gon!
Love is a thyng as any spirit free.
Wommen, of kynde, desiren libertee,
And nat to been constreyned as a thral;
And so doon men, if I sooth seyen shal.

F. 764–770.

Jean de Meun's lines about the restlessness of women here find their counterpart and answer. Dignity, freedom, respectful affection, are implicitly accorded to the sex by Chaucer's words; for he is here dealing chiefly, it must be remembered, with wedded love. On his reform tendencies, I remark elsewhere that Chaucer "spreads the contagious propaganda of a kindly view of human nature," and I may now observe that this extends to women. How often he reflects the difficulties of the domestic scene, but never with rancor! Pertelote in the *Nun's Priest's Tale* offers troublesome advice, in wifely fashion, to Chantecler, and Chantecler quotes the old diatribes against women: "Mulier est hominis confusio." Yet he sugars the pill and butters his bread at the same time; and the relation between magnificent husband and solicitous if domineering wife continues well enough in the story. There are wives who betray husbands, but there are others who do not. The Wife of Bath shows a militant suffragist rampant for her rights; but she gives away her exaggerated case even as she argues for it, and the Clerk and the others of the group furnish the corrective. Chaucer's humor, therefore, on the problem of the woman question is not fundamentally satiric; it is again a part of his healthy attitude toward life based on a sense of proportion with the seasoning of wisdom. *Mulier est hominis confusio*, true enough; but the other side of the medal is that woman is man's joy and all his bliss. It is like the two inscriptions of the gate leading to the garden of Love in the *Parliament*. These things are not simple.

Of specific allusions to the great traditions of chivalry, the *service des dames*, the *dolce styl nuovo*, Chaucer shows surprisingly few. There is something of the sort in the picture of the knight in black who mourns the death of Blanche the Duchess; again there is something in the eagles all ready to do battle for the formel in the *Parliament*; and in the *Canterbury Tales* there is Sir Thopas galloping forth for love of a lady bright whom he has yet to meet, there are Palamon and Arcite doing battle for a lady who knows nothing of their existence, and there is the knight who rapes a lady and is punished for it. Chivalry indeed is at a low ebb during that moment in the poet's maturity when he wrote of the knight in bed with his wedded wife as follows:

> He walweth and he turneth to and fro.
> His olde wyf lay smylynge everemo,
> And seyde, "O deere housbonde, *benedicitee*!
> Fareth every knyght thus with his wyf as ye?
> Is this the lawe of kyng Arthures hous?
> Is every knyght of his so dangerous?"
>
> D. 1085–1090.

The ennobling power of love is reflected in the *Troilus*, and the *Squire's Tale* seems to show flashes from the brilliance of former days of chivalry in such phrases as that of "Gawayn, with his olde curteisye," and the allusion to Lancelot.

But there seems to be no slightest trace of evidence that Chaucer thought about all these things as a problem — as, for example, he did, I believe, cogitate about the significance of dreams, and the paradox of free will and divine foresight. The status of woman, then, was not for him an academic question for which he had an answer ready. All his attention in such matters was fixed upon women as human beings, engaged in ordinary activities, living and breathing in their various classes of society, occupied with the virtues or weaknesses of their preference, and withal intensely human. If the poet approached the question at all, he approached it empirically. He took notes in this regard from authorities and also from personal observation of life. It may be remembered that of all his characters those which are most fit for canonization are women; his most contemptible rogues are among the men. On the other hand, his saintly women are those that derive least from real life, and seem to be held as less delightful than exemplary.

Where among all of Chaucer's portraits of women is there anyone of the stature and dignity of the great ladies of virtue assuredly available to his genius? Shakespeare has a host of them, varying in temperament and ability, like Hermione, Desdemona, both Portias, the Helena of *All's Well*, Rosalind, Beatrice, and the rest, some witty and perverse, others calm and reserved, but all clearly set forth with a serene integrity. Despite the implications of the Prologue of the *Legend*, I assume that in royalty and elsewhere in the fourteenth century a few ladies, at least, could have been seen like these; I do not believe that feminine virtue was on the upward grade for the first time in the sixteenth century.

Chaucer must have known something about Queen Philippa; there were the Duchess Blanche and John of Gaunt's
second wife, Constance of Castile. In literature too there
were at least the Beatrice of Dante, Chrétien's Enid, Lau-
dine, and Lunet, Gottfried's and Thomas's Brengwain, and
various afflicted ladies in the Constance saga and the story of
St Eustace who protected their virtue and their children.
There were besides these certain characters in allegory, like
Dame Nature, Prudence, Fame, and even the Philosophia of
Boethius, who suggest the dignity of educated women and
their wisdom. Chaucer gives us some of these; he does retell the story of Constance, with a glance, I have no doubt,
at the personal holiness of John of Gaunt's second wife. But
in all his writings I find hardly more than two good women
who stand out as richly characterized and important and
clear. Of course he does very well by Dame Nature in the
Parliament, and by Fame in the poem devoted to her. I am
also ready to admit that Griselda approaches the distinction
I have in mind, especially when she shows her human weakness in her curiosity to see the Marquis's new wife and again
(later in the story) his second wife, and in her touch of rebelliousness. But even here Chaucer does not show the
power of invention, the vitality of realism, which he has for
his less admirable ladies, and which we expect from him
when his imagination is stirred. I find him inspired in that
way only twice in his work, in the case of Blanche the
Duchess and again with the Prioress. Griselda, Constance,
Dorigen, look in the same direction no doubt; but the portraits of Blanche and the Prioress are done at full length.

Although the description of Blanche is a composite according to the best methods of the Manuals of Rhetoric, its details are carefully chosen and I for one find the lady a living creature in this elegy. She not only teaches the torches to burn bright; she is herself the torch from which all may borrow light. As Cressid's eyes implied "What, may I not stand here?" so hers told each friend of pardon and peace. She exceeds all, it is true, in beauty and virtue; but unlike the heroines of romance she does not send her suitors on a wild-goose chase to Tartary. Conventional as is most of the material, from her golden hair to her faultless figure, there are certain points that give her reality: "Hyr lokynge was not foly sprad," her speech was healing, "pure suffraunt was hir wyt," and her wit itself was set "Without malyce, upon gladnesse." Among ten thousand she would have been "chef myrour of al the feste." How rich in connotation that expression is! Contrast Machaut's phrase which was its source:

> M'estoit miroir et exemplaire
> De tous biens desirer et faire.
>> *Remede de Fortune*, 171–172.

A good idea is here borrowed from the French poet and touched with a wand. So the whole picture is radiant with power. In the languor of the dream, and in the somber avowal of Chaucer's knight in black, the poet makes us see the graciousness, the poise, and the detachment of the Duchess; somehow the inventory of her charms does what it was meant to do. Even in the portrait, as so often in other literary forms, Chaucer gives life to the conventional.

But presumably it is a portrait. One would like to know whether the same is true of the Prioress. Here again much has been borrowed from sources but all is wisely chosen. Here, and as her story proceeds, the nun emerges as a great lady more realistically presented than Blanche, and — except that in her repressions perhaps or in the single focus of her dedication she may seem less of a person — as clear as the Wife of Bath. Only a reader who feels that under strict discipline personality ceases to flower can regard her as unimportant. She has attained a position of special honor in her community, and, if we may judge from her present outlook and purpose, she holds it successfully. She has a personal distinction in manners and in bearing. She does not speak out like the Parson to rebuke worldliness, but she does rebuke by implication the monks who are not as holy as they should be. The beginning of Chaucer's portraits is always significant: the Knight is worthy, the Monk is "a fair for the maistrie," the Friar is wanton and merry, the Clerk has recourse to logic, the Lawyer is "war and wys," the Wife of Bath is deaf, the Parson rich in holy thought and work, the Reeve slender and choleric. These are not casual touches; the note is struck at once. In the case of the Prioress what we see first is her smile, "simple and coy." But here "coy" does not mean coquettish; rather she seems to have the gracious charm of various ladies in romance and allegory of whom the same phrase is used, and her smile is reserved. A bit later in the description we read that she was:

> . . . ful plesaunt, and amyable of port,
> And peyned hire to countrefete cheere
> Of court, and to been estatlich of manere,
> And to ben holden digne of reverence.
>
> A. 138–141.

The ideas go together. I cannot discover that the Parson ever wore a smile; he would have told a better story if he had. But the Prioress does know something of humor; and it may be her manners or her notion of dignity, rather than her conception of the religious life, that tends to make her narrow. It is this sense of humor combined with sensibility, with her childless life, and with the imperfect satisfactions that a person of her temperament (for she is certainly not a saint) may find in the world of religion, that gives us, not merely the little clergeoun of her story but also, her own matchless portrait exquisite in its delicacy.

Mr. Lowes has seen in her the "engagingly imperfect submergence of the feminine in the ecclesiastical." Sister Madeleva on the contrary finds in her a "picture of a woman a decade or more beyond middle age . . . sweetened and spiritually transformed by the rules and religious practises of her choice, who can be in the world without being of it, gracious without affectation, and friendly without boldness." I am not sure that the Prioress would not have been immeasurably gratified at producing just these different impressions on a modern man and a modern nun. Well, I admit I find her fascinating; but I catch certain overtones of worldliness in the description — in the sensibility, in her manners, in the little dogs, even in the brooch with all its religious associations. That we cannot be sure with Sister Madeleva about how old Madame Eglantine is, may be regarded as natural, considering the fact that most nuns in their wimples are decidedly of an uncertain age. That there is so sharp a difference of interpretation of the portrait, that the truth probably lies — not somewhere between the two but — in both ideas, suggests that we have here something like objective creation rather than vagueness, a creation that plays back and forth between various temperaments, something of the worldly, something of the heavenly, like a living human being. In comparison the Wife of Bath is static. Moreover if this picture changes its meaning, from the interpretation of Mr. Lowes to that of Sister Madeleva, according to the light by which it is read, or gets an iridescence from both, we may find in it an embodiment of the Christian attitude toward woman, touched by the secular tradition of the Court of Love. *"Amor vincit omnia!"* *"Which of the two loves does 'amor' mean to the Prioress?"* asks Mr. Lowes, and adds at once, "I do not know; but I think she thought she meant love celestial." Now let us be as gracious as the Host and pay our respects to this lady of dignity; we may be certain that at least part of the time she *did* mean love celestial. The Wife of Bath has sometimes been proclaimed as the anticipation of the modern woman with all her freedoms. However that may be, to the Middle Ages she was merely the old Eve reincarnate; the Prioress was truly the new woman, at once human and also dignified in her virtue.

Chapter VI

THE CANTERBURY TALES

WHEN CHAUCER'S pilgrims set forth for Canterbury, sap was running, and in the tops of the hedgerows appeared green shoots, the new season was on tiptoe and promise was restless in the air. One can dilate on these things at some length, but it is hardly necessary. It had been done in numerous passages on spring long before Chaucer's day, and so many sources have been suggested for the opening passage of the *General Prologue* that it is quite clear no special borrowing is likely to be identified. The point that may be missed is that sap was running not only in the trees and bushes but also in the pilgrims; there is a kind of emotional turbulence visible in the travelers to Becket's shrine that is not sufficiently explained by their holy purpose. The Pardoner is moved to lay bare his inmost hypocrisies and yet falls into others as he does so; the Canon's Yeoman issues a declaration of independence; the Miller and the Reeve, the Friar and the Summoner fight; the Wife of Bath goes in for a great debauch of exhibitionism and stirs a whole group of pilgrims to discuss her theories at least by implication; and there is much more ado. In fact I believe that, if the poet had got round to it, he would have displayed a quarrel between the Merchant and the Lawyer, the Nun's Priest and the Physician. I can give evidence to this effect. A pilgrimage, like life itself, has many opportunities this side its goal. It was just the season and just the enterprise for a dramatic poet.

As the poet visits the Tabard, moreover, we can be certain that he sees the people he wants to see, characters who will have the greatest offering in terms of characterization. For this was Chaucer's specialty. He cannot, and perhaps he would not, find royalty there; such a thing would be unrealistic and also indiscreet. Not that the portrayal of royalty, perhaps one should insist nowadays, would be more impoverished than that of other classes, the gentry, the bourgeoisie, or even the proletariat, as we can tell from glimpses in *Troilus and Criseyde*, the *Knight's Tale*, and elsewhere. Nobility in rank is perhaps reflected as much in the *Nun's Priest's Tale* as in the *Parliament of Fowls*. But the poet could not have had royalty sharing in the give and take of the pilgrimage. Except then for the special virtues of the Court, we may expect to find in the travelers to the great shrine those qualities of mankind that most engaged the poet's attention, and in a way his comment thereon. Again we may possibly observe what he likes and what he cares less for, what he sadly accepts and what he regards as amusing.

In the catalogue of the pilgrims the dignity of the Knight leads off. It is dignity, however, combined with "meekness," and yet a meekness which did not hold for the century the insipid idea indicated by the word to-day. It is also combined with undoubted valor, and with marked simplicity of dress and manner. The pilgrims whom Chaucer seems to find most admirable are touched with a fine simplicity — the Clerk, the Parson, and the Plowman: which, we quickly add, is not to say that necessarily he liked them best. In fact the Parson and the Plowman may have been idealized for moral purposes. I may confess that in the latter I find a startling touch of something like nineteenth-century romanticism, as if the poet had seen plowmen from a distance and in his image of them was mingled the wholesome savor of the earth. I fear that in these descriptions the material moves neither in the direction of what was typical nor in that of what was realistic. The dignity of the Knight is a little offset by the mention of his "worthinesse," as if he too is an honorable man in the sense that the Franklin is a worthy vavasour. But if his respectability is pushed a little, it is managed with delicacy, like the kindliness of saying that "He was a verray, parfit, gentil knight." The Clerk and the Parson show traces of ascetic living as well as of unsparing diligence; the Plowman carts many a load of manure while his heart is filled with love of God and his fellow-men. Diligence, benignity, clean-living, mercy, fairness, these are virtues that run through these men and seem to show the poet's approval.

In general the women do not fare quite so well, and perhaps the best types were not to be discovered on a pilgrimage. Apparently there are but three; one is obscure, and the Prioress stands out as far as morality is concerned. As I have implied in the preceding chapter, she has her vanities, even in the elegance which she borrows like a jewel for celestial purposes from the *Roman de la Rose*. As the story of the Knight reveals him as richer in humor than one might have supposed, and as the *Clerk's Tale* uncovers depths of slyness we might not have suspected in the scholar, so the Prioress has a narrative that does her vast credit as a woman of religion. Here we see that she knows love celestial, even if pilgrims and critics who read her brooch think otherwise. In feminine terms, she too is essentially worthy.

The Squire and the Franklin Chaucer seems also to find without great blemish. The Squire is just what a proper young man of the upper classes should be, physically well endowed, with flexibility and abundant vigor. His vanities do not do him discredit, his fashionable clothes with the embroidery and long wide sleeves, his poetry and his passion. Doubtless his religion that prompts him to go to Canterbury has much that is theoretical about it still. His thoughts will be with his lady; only his years have so far kept him "unspotted from the world," and that I mean aesthetically rather than morally. His charm is nature's giving; he is as "fressh as is the month of May," and any young animal has grace. Besides he too has done well on military expeditions, and he has carved "biforn his fader at the table." How these points add to the background! The pilgrimage so often gives us this fourth dimension, a touch of the drama in the lives of these characters off stage. So we hear of the Host's negotiations with his stormy wife, of the Merchant's frustrated love, and of the Franklin's disappointment in his son who is not, we see, on the road to Canterbury. The Franklin may represent a type to which the poet owes much gratitude for hearty hospitality. He loads his tables and piles on the food. It snows in his house with meat and drink. No one can object to that. He is St Julian in his own country; far from being without honor he too is worthy. Chaucer's son Thomas was once called a St Julian.

We cannot be so sure of the harmlessness of the Merchant and the Lawyer. Except for social reasons, one might consider them along with the Manciple and the Reeve. All four show a rather hard interior. The Merchant is gracious enough, but he makes sure of his winnings. Business is business when it comes to the exchange. His unfortunate marriage, of which we hear when we come to his story, may have made him bitter in all his dealings. His violent frustration has turned in on himself, and his satiric portrait of January is wormwood for his own savoring. In contrast the Franklin's grief is for his son, and even that is set aside in the mellow outlook revealed in his story; there everyone, squire and all, gets a prize. Good food has not made him dyspeptic, because he shares it liberally. The Merchant, however, keeps his own counsel; and though he too is one of the worthies, his mordant aim is ever for himself. As for the Lawyer, like all the rest, he is the best of his kind, no one can catch him amiss, he makes a great show of being busy but we know little about what goes on his mind. His story of Constance was evidently not assigned to him at first; perhaps Chaucer was not sure what sort of narrative would fit a man of such dignity. What sort of yarn would the historical Pynchbek relate? Would he have felt an unconscious sympathy for the much beleaguered Constance amid so many ruthless foes, as a selfish man who has suspicions and fears of his own and has escaped from one conspiracy only to be attacked by another? Or would he (like the Monk with his hundred tragedies) suppose that telling a story so piteous would impress others with his greatness of soul?

The Manciple and the Reeve butter their own bread even more firmly. The poet likes their efficiency, and even their cleverness; but they are not appealing figures. Most people are afraid of the Reeve "as of the deeth," though he has a nice house and does his job well. The meagerness of his person suits his meager spirit. Like the Wife of Bath he has a colt's tooth. "Yet in our asshen olde is fyr yreke" (A. 3882); still in his ashes live their wonted fires! But he speaks bare truth when he says that his stream of life has almost run out and the old tun is almost empty; whereas the Wife of Bath has not entirely lost her pith, no matter what she says. He and the Manciple are both cheats, and both tell stories of cuckoldry.

But if we are going in for rascals there are better than both on the pilgrimage, and I feel it likely that Chaucer found the Monk better company. For one thing the Monk surrounded himself with more agreeable living: like the Prioress he has sensibility, but that is because he likes pleasant sensations of every sort. Soft fur is comfortable to the wrists, supple boots to the feet, and a fat swan to the palate; so he delights even in the feeling of piety, and that is why he became a monk and that is why he tells his succession of pathetic stories. The love-knot he wears might indicate that he would admit the soft impeachment of the Host were Harry Bailey's charge not so indelicate. It may be unfair to call him a rascal when his self-indulgences are so far on the side of what is childish — his insistence on comfort despite his vows, and his hunting, the jangling bells, a chiefly innocent kind of entertainment. Like a child he is vexed when his pious stories are stopped; he will not go on. This "manly man" like some others shows, as the saying is or should be, that he "has the heart of a child."

The Friar is even better. There may be more cheating here, but there is less self-deception. His popularity with the "worthy women" of the town is a sign in his favor quite as much as it is a giveaway. He is likeable; in some sort he is dependable. All the innuendoes regarding the way he hears confession and gives absolution and makes marriages at his own cost do not spoil this point. He is one of those people whom nature has blessed with charm; he has a way with him and knows it. If we forget (and there were some people in the fourteenth century who did not find the task difficult) that he was under vows to be a follower of St Francis of Assisi, we cannot help delighting in his company. His vanities, his white neck (full proof that he goes with the aristocracy rather than with the poor), his lisp to make his English sweet upon his tongue, his songs, his expert knowledge of the taverns, seem virtues. He tells a masterly story. Let us therefore overlook his neglect of the poor and his cultivation of the rich! His friend the Monk followed the new mode in things spiritual, enjoyed the good things of this world waiting for the next — and we said he had the right idea ("And I seyde his opinioun was good!"): after all, why not? And so the Friar fills a long felt want, especially with the ladies, and is cheerful with everybody. Why does Chaucer seem to like him? — but Chaucer likes everybody in due measure, except perhaps the Pardoner. He does not forget, be it noticed, to record the sin; but he likes the sinner. And the Friar has not only charm but great vitality.

These two characteristics engage the poet's attention elsewhere. I pass over the Shipman, the Doctor, the Miller, and the others, who in various ways illustrate qualities that I think Chaucer found especially significant. But there are two of his portraits over which anyone must pause, that of the

Wife of Bath and that of the Pardoner, both rascals in their way and both drawn on a large canvas. In the Wife of Bath we have again great vitality and charm; in the Pardoner we have also a kind of perverse vitality and perverted charm. The Wife, as everyone knows, is a superb creation. She is a world, God's plenty, all in herself. One can go on romanticizing about her as the eternal creative impulse, the unleashed instinct of womanhood, emancipated *joie de vivre*, and what not. I pause because for the moment I cannot recall the rest of the liturgy in praise of Eros. The Wife, however, is not an admirable figure when it comes to instruction or idealism; she cannot be taken as a leader in social reform, as I seem to remember one modern critic has contended. Nor did Chaucer regard her as the honest propagandist of a set of new moral standards. Her pretensions, her sophistries, are familiar in countless instances before her day; but (and this is the real point) not with her utterance or her voice.

Profane, obscene, she shouts at everybody. And why not? — she is deaf, and she is also of the type that thinks noise means revelry and mirth. She has vast laughter, and ruthless inclusiveness. She must gather into her circle everyone within reach, jab this one in the ribs, chuck another under the chin, yell hoarsely at a third. She has the ecclesiasts purple with rage or with unseemly mirth. She stands (so she thinks) the quiet Clerk on his head. Her vanities are great and conspicuous, her big headdress, her mantle about her huge hips, her red stockings. She is of the sort that to achieve distinction outdoes the fashions; but there is just a drop of pathos in the way this kind of person vainly throws the ball a mile beyond first base and loses the game. She is a galleon under

full sail, she is a veritable carack broad in the beam and leading the wind. Blake's portrait is nothing like her, because
with all her grossness she is not a caricature. Stothard's is
deficient because it has not the torrent of her blood within
its veins. She is not a person to emulate or to avoid; simply
we cannot keep our eyes off her. She is hearty humanity un-
redeemed. Life is scarcely a problem for anyone like her who
takes it with such a colossal welcome. She wants her body
full of it, and more in readiness. She has the print of Saint
Venus's seal without the beauty of the goddess; she is the
eternal feminine but not that which leads upward to the
celestial. In other words she is sheer energy without any of
the more poetic or spiritual qualities which might attenuate
it. Even when she does protest with a tear that age has withered her a bit and custom staled, we know that she has an
eye for a sixth husband whenever he comes in sight. God
bless him, what exercise he will get!

Her energy shows as much in her command of pathos as
in her other types of emotional appeal:

> "But age, allas! that al wole envenyme,
> Hath me biraft my beautee and my pith.
> Lat go, farewel! the devel go therwith!"
>
> D. 474–476.

Her confession of the duplicity of women is like the Pardoner's brief moment of honesty, and about as sincere:

> "For half so boldely kan ther no man
> Swere and lyen, as a womman kan.
> I sey nat this by wyves that been wyse,
> But if it be whan they hem mysavyse.

A wys wyf shal, if that she kan hir good,
Bere hym on honde that the cow (chough) is wood,
And take witnesse of hir owene mayde
Of hir assent. . . ."

D. 227–234.

In other words, the wise wife will deceive her husband by
saying that the talkative chough who gives her away (in the
manner of the bird in the *Manciple's Tale*) is crazy. The Wife
of Bath is enjoying her own candor at this point, and her own
freedom from self-deceit. But there is little sadness in her
Prologue, or in her story when she gets to it; her nature is
too healthy for that type of expression, and frustration with
her will be taken out in rage or blows.

"My fifthe housbonde, God his soule blesse!
Which that I took for love, and no richesse,"

D. 525–526.

— an expression of genuine feeling, but she is soon telling
how she tricked and exposed him.

All these traits suggest strength. But her overflow of energy is not entirely a matter of superabundance. Seen from
the Parson's angle her indiscriminate outpouring is defiant.
Her Prologue is a long defense. She is arguing a case against
a thousand critics of whom she is conscious, pausing now and
then to pat herself on the back, to ridicule the Clerk, or to
show her own skill. There is much in the zeal of her exhibitionism to suggest weakness to the modern psychologist.
So much talk about her success in Love's dance, her colt's
tooth and her other resources, reveals a concern in these
matters. She is a furnace of energy, but the fires are not so
bright as they used to be. She is slowing up apace and knows

it. She has had her world in her time; but her weakness shows in the fact that she takes this as memory and is telling about it. If the apple has passed its prime, what are we to do about it? If we are afraid of the future, we stall, throw dust in the air, challenge everybody within reach to see how lusty we are, try by fair means or foul to gain time, and incidentally overwhelm anyone who will listen to our harangue. No, the Wife of Bath is not all strength!

Nor is the uncomely Pardoner all weakness. His is a despised condition. His high-pitched voice told men what was the matter with him, however much he boasted of having a jolly wench in every town. His companionship with the horrible Summoner in the song "Come hider, love, to me" is the most violent satire in all of Chaucer's poetry. The insinuation shows the poet's hatred. The Pardoner's vanities are all repulsive — he wears no hood "for jolitee," and his hair falls in hanks; his own picture of himself preaching, stretching his neck and bobbing his head like a dove on a barn, is grotesque; his pardons come all hot from Rome, and these with his fake relics suggest the worst abuses of religion. And like the Wife of Bath's Prologue his own fairly long discourse is all defense. He is insecure at many points where he must summon evidence of his skill, his insight, his shrewdness, his power to swindle men, his way with women, and his innate and genuine (so he would urge) if not generally recognized piety. On this latter point he will confess, he says, that Christ after all is best. Oh, yes, he too can be honest if need be! Most piercingly sad of all perhaps, when we remember his condition, is the hardened bluff involved when he interrupts the Wife of Bath:

"Now, dame," quod he, "by God and by seint John!
Ye been a noble prechour in this cas.
I was aboute to wedde a wyf; allas!
What sholde I bye it on my flessh so deere?
Yet hadde I levere wedde no wyf to-yeere!"

                        D. 164–168.

But while all this shows profound weakness and insecurity, there is little doubt that the Pardoner knows he is a crook. He produced the fake relics. He knows that he bamboozles the crowd with manifold and skilful appeals. Outwardly he is a hypocrite; but inwardly he runs a risk of being a cheat with himself only when he is trying to be "honest" with the pilgrims. If he really thought that Christ was best, thought it with his whole nature, his life would be different; but his is the dishonesty of the person who says "I wish I could be religious!"

In contrast the Wife of Bath tries zealously to persuade herself that her argument runs fairly, and that she is an emancipated woman above all poor deluded females, that her way of life is right and acceptable for all sensible folk, and that she is happier than anyone else and more honest besides. The wretched Pardoner seldom fools himself in this way or tries to do so. That is his strength. He is right in thinking he can fool all the people all of the time, and he is justified in taking his satisfactions in that narrow vein. It is the best he has left. On the other hand, the Wife's satisfactions are mainly social. She has liked people and been undoubtedly liked in return. She has real friendships. I fear the Pardoner has none. I fear that his existence is taken up with a solitary concern for himself, the desperate concern of the man who

lives by deceiving mankind and who has only the dark satisfaction of his pride. This must necessarily grow more and
more juiceless as he is more and more cut off from his kind
by treachery. As Mr. Kittredge has observed, he is a "lost
soul," and a definite indication of the fact is that Geoffrey
Chaucer has so little mercy on him. Chaucer's most unsparing couplet in all his works is that in which he makes the
Pardoner say:

> "Thus spitte I out my venym under hewe
> Of hoolynesse, to semen hooly and trewe."
>   C. 421–422.

And so with deceit in his pleasures, his profession, his idealism and religion, and even in his humor, the Pardoner has
that isolation which is Hell. But his strength in the endurance
of such a life is obviously, like a saint's, heroic. The Wife of
Bath in her scurrilous remarks that include Church and religion and saint can never effect the blasphemy that the Pardoner himself embodies; beside him in this respect she is
feeble.

Incidentally in these figures Chaucer shows his own preju-
dice about what is forgivable. The Wife is forgiven, not
because she loved much but because of her fundamental and
hearty kindliness. In the Pardoner there is none of this; in
him we see what the poet felt about holiness and men who
betrayed it. Now it is not wholly frivolous to inquire which
among all the pilgrims, rascals and redeemed, Chaucer
would have chosen not merely for companionship but for
intimacy. He would have drunk his drink, I am sure, with
any of them. But in which would he have found his Horatio

or Mercutio? Certainly not the Knight or the Parson or the Plowman as matters stand. Them he would respect no doubt but seldom turn to for one of his asides. The Squire he would watch with amusement; the Prioress and her aides he would offer the right kind of homage, as indeed he would any ecclesiast except the Pardoner. Yet we may remember that it is Chaucer who sees Madame Eglantine's vanities; that when the Knight interrupts the Monk and the Host ventures his obscene impudence, it is the poet who has done all this; and that when the Summoner and the Friar have their fight and tell their fabliaux, it is he again who sees them in this way. One may go through the whole pilgrimage and find the poet representing his company with balanced judgment; but from them all he stands artistically aloof. Dignity, benignity, diligence, bountiful generosity, simplicity, these are the virtues he likes in the men who have them. Plain energy and charm he relishes wherever he finds them. The rascals with outgoing natures and less pretence he likes, as he allows full value to the Friar's easy ways and the Miller's thumb. But among them all we do not find exactly his compeer and trusted friend. Is this because his best friend was of royal station and so not among those present, or because here we have the reflection of a man who always went home when the day's work was done, to study or cogitate in his own company?

How much unhappiness there is echoed in the overtones of what these pilgrims have known in the world at large! The Host's domestic misery as well as the Merchant's; the hard money-getting of Merchant, Lawyer, Manciple, and Reeve; the painful industry or unremitting toil of the Clerk,

the Parson, and the Plowman; the poignant and hopeless solitude of the Pardoner; the cheating, brawling, drunken debauchery so often pictured in the stories with the smell of
mortality; the great succession of amours hinted at or revealed in the cases of the Monk and Friar, Summoner,
Pardoner, and Wife of Bath, in which the stench of flesh prevails rather than the grace of Eros — all these features like
the Great Plague more than once mentioned tell of a perilous, unlovely existence which were better avoided in a flight
from reality. Yet such a flight Chaucer did not take. He not
only worked in the Custom House — one could escape from
that contact as Hawthorne did centuries later — but he obviously carried reality in his head. Even in his early poems, his
allegories, his imagination keeps darting back for bits of ordinary experience, like the expression in the eyes of the
Duchess, the description of the glimpse of earth as seen from
the eagle's clutch, the fish in the pool in the garden of love;
compared with French analogues Chaucer's poems of
Courtly Love are realistic. I am certain the poet did not flee
from mankind in any morbid isolation, though he did return home at night with relief and sought his book.

Of all the pilgrims who might have been congenial to him
I suggest the Clerk as most likely, in his precise wit and in
his reticence. We remember the poet's allusion in the *House
of Fame* and in the *Legend* to his own studying. Everywhere
he proves it in his complicated use of source material. His
silence after the pathos of the *Prioress's Tale*, and his breaking forth, on being challenged, with the raucous gaiety of
the story of Sir Thopas, furnish a remote parallel to the
Clerk's silence under the discipline of the Wife of Bath and

his ultimate revenge. But the Clerk, be it said, is no Chaucer.
He is too exclusively Aristotelian for one thing; his library
includes nothing of the Court of Love, no romances, no
poetry, no nonsense of any sort. He would not lend an ear
to the naughty Friar; he would have had no patience for the
Pardoner or the Wife of Bath. To the latter, I fear, Chaucer
would have occasionally turned for a story or a bit of gossip;
as he once fell in love with Criseyde, now he would find
diversion in the Wife of Bath and the infidelities which are
her glory. She is a bonfire that kindles heat rather than light;
but it does warm the hands and heart. Where in life may one
find the perfect embodiment of all we long for: warmth of
living, dignity of mind, exaltation of soul? Take it here and
there as you may, but give yourself to no single example,
Clerk or Wife of Bath, or any other! After it is over, go back
to your room for purposes of contemplation. If the pilgrimage does reach the shrine of Becket, no one will be told exactly what happened there. At least the Clerk and Chaucer
are unlikely to speak out.

With the many ecclesiasts on this pilgrimage it is strange
that so little is said of religion. Of morality, yes, in the discreet advice of the *Tale of Melibeus* and the *Parson's Tale*,
and in the indiscretions of many pilgrims. Piety shines in the
awkward enthusiasm of the story of St Cecilia, and freely
in the martyrdom of the little Clergeoun. But where is anything shown like the writings of Richard Rolle of Hampole,
or those of Dame Juliana of Norwich, or the *Cloud of Un-
knowing*? Here is a type of medieval literature Chaucer does
not include, and not because prose was unfitted to his framework. Visionary experiences would have had even a dramatic

value, especially if, as he managed with several other confessions, he could have persuaded a religious of a more exalted temperament to let himself or herself go. His pilgrims show no reluctance to pour out their hearts; there were fourteenth-century mystics (like Margery Kempe later) who traveled considerably and one of them might have divulged his or her mysteries. But it may be that understanding of this kind of experience is something Chaucer did not share. He read and knew Dante's *Paradiso*, he quotes it, and we must believe he finished reading it; but what he thought of the vision of the Triune God in rings of light he does not say, and there is no sign in the pilgrimage that he himself sought to peer, however darkly, in that direction.

At most we can say that there is fervor in the closing passage of the *Troilus*, and perhaps a mystical quality in his renderings of St Bernard's prayer to the Virgin. The latter he used in the prologue to the *Second Nun's Tale* and again in that of the *Prioress's Tale*. Let me quote from them in that order, which is probably the order of composition:

> Thow Mayde and Mooder, doghter of thy Sone,
> Thow welle of mercy, synful soules cure,
> In whom that God for bountee chees to wone,
> Thow humble, and heigh over every creature,
> Thow nobledest so ferforth oure nature,
> That no desdeyn the Makere hadde of kynde
> His Sone in blood and flessh to clothe and wynde.
>
> G. 36–42.

> O mooder Mayde! O mayde Mooder free!
> O bussh unbrent, brennynge in Moyses sighte,
> That ravyshedest doun fro the Deitee

Thurgh thyn humblesse, the Goost that in th'alighte,
Of whos vertu, whan he thyn herte lighte,
Conceyved was the Fadres sapience,
Help me to telle it in thy reverence!

                    B. 1657–1663.

In the second version the lines sing. The artist it is, no doubt, who has heightened the feeling here, and even made it violent in figure. No doubt too the poet might suppose that the Prioress would be more gifted in speech than the Second Nun. But it was Chaucer himself, though he rearranged the lines from Dante and added other touches, who could not forget the marvel of the original prayer. It cannot be said that a great poet never repeats himself; but it is certainly true that when he does, there is significance in the fact. Thus Chaucer gives expression in *Gentilesse* to ideas that also appear in the disquisition in the *Wife of Bath's Tale* on true nobility. Obviously he had pondered on the thought that "unto vertu longeth dignitee" (*Gentilesse*, 5). Then he incorporated a long discourse on the subject in the bedroom scene of the Wife's narrative, and put it on the lips of the loathly lady. I suppose he meant it, but like an unwilling moralist he scampered away from it by giving it the comic setting (as in truth he also put the *Tale of Melibeus* where it is in the *Canterbury Tales*). In the case of the prayer to Our Lady, however, in each instance its setting is what it should be; indeed like devotional candles at a shrine it is a worthy prelude to the subsequent legend. I like to think of Chaucer's reading St Bernard's prayer in the *Paradiso* and of his reading it again and again. The lines obviously did not leave his memory.

But if there is little of the mystical in Chaucer's verse there is much of the ostensibly religious. We remember Chaucer translated the *ABC.* of De Guileville; he retold (not much inspired) the story of St Cecilia; he gives us what is almost a saint's legend in the *Prioress's Tale*; and the stories of Constance and Griselda are not far removed from this *genre*. "Paradoxical as it seems to us," observed Mr. Kittredge, "Chaucer must have ranked high as a religious writer." Much of his writing in this vein is in the seven-line stanza, and I have been tempted at times to classify the poet's work into periods based on moods: poetry of love, on the heights, disillusion, and the like (as we used to divide Shakespeare's career); but it does not work out properly. The moods appear and reappear in one another's domain; Chaucer was not a victim primarily of this or that disposition, and what tended to guide him was literary fashion or his sources — that is if anything can be said to have dictated his style or subject matter. But I wonder occasionally whether in the late seventies he did not have a special preoccupation with religious material; whether perhaps he did not have the plan of collecting stories of really good women and Christian saints — like Constance, Griselda, Cecilia, and the little martyr. If this is the case we must add the story of Virginia: it speaks of Nature as vicar of the Lord and is thus reminiscent of the *Parliament of Fowls*. Yet its reference to corrupt governesses and its couplet seem to place it in 1386 or thereabouts. Incidentally it would appear that Chaucer thought highly of it: its emotional effect on the pilgrims would apparently place it next to the *Prioress's Tale*, and that is compliment enough.

Most of these stories are less religious than they are moral. They are like case histories of virtue in operation; there is this much truth in the theory once offered by Professor F. L. Tupper that in the *Canterbury Tales* Chaucer dealt schematically with the Seven Deadly Sins. It may be true that a realistic writer can hardly tell stories without treating of the Sins in some way or other, but in this group we come rather close at times to personified virtue at her virtuous task. It may almost be said that when the poet deals with virtue he is usually academic: in his theory as in the *Parson's Tale*, and in his instances of it. But the characters after all do escape from being two-dimensional; Chaucer, as I have observed, does not seem to care for personified abstraction. So we do have the grief of Constance for her child, the moment of rebelliousness in Griselda, Cecilia's slanging the Judge, Virginia's reluctance to die. Weakness of one kind or another is the third dimension that carries these creatures into life and is their saving grace. Here I suspect is the clue to Chaucer's personal interest in these plots: less than the holiness of these ladies it is the incongruity of their weakness (that is to say their humanity) that counted with his genius, although of course its value is derived from the background of virtue.

But I have also another idea as to what Chaucer found appealing in these stories and led him to retell them. This suggestion I put forth timidly, aware as I am that critics of a certain important stamp will reject the notion as preposterous. Nevertheless with some degree of assurance I may say that what attracted Chaucer in almost every case was an element in the plot that may only be described as comic. The word has, of course, a variety of meanings and I may be rash in

using it here. To a reader weak in humor it means something
clumsy — burlesque perhaps, a touch of the gross which
the highest form of art (though he will admit, the same cannot be said for the highest form of artist) will not tolerate.
Obviously I mean none of these things when I speak of the
comic in these stories. But properly speaking the word may
also imply something gentle and even tender, something
allied to that vein of sympathetic irony which has been noted
in the poet's works, the product of a living sense of humorous values not at all discreditable to its possessor. I see it in the
story of Constance in her endless navigations in the rudder-
less boat, in Cecilia's grim hold on chastity with the help of
an angel (I know the puritan will part company from me
here) and in her slanging the Judge, in Griselda's dauntless
stability of character, and most exquisitely of all in the little
Clerk's persistent singing with his throat cut:

> "My throte is kut unto my nekke boon,"
> Seyde this child . . .
>   B. 1839–1840

and I know he said it exultantly. They simply could not stop
his singing. He went on and on until they got the grain from
his tongue. Mirth, if that is the word for it, is intrinsic in the
episode, but it is like a smile on Our Lady's face as she hears
the unceasing *"Alma redemptoris* everemo!"

We shall be told that all this represents nothing better than
reading modern ideas and a modern sense of proportion into
a fourteenth-century poet, and that from our point of view
practically all medieval legends include the ridiculous. But
the legends vary in this matter. And on the first point I in-

sist that good sense goes far back into the history of man and so does a sense of proportion. In particular it may be pointed out that Chaucer himself shows that he perceived the humor implicit in Griselda's patience by the dramatic framework in which he placed the tale, and in a special sense by the Envoy. "Grisilde is deed, and eek hire pacience!" Comparable to this eternal "sadnesse" of Griselda is the obstinacy with which Cecilia resists death in the bath of fire (she did not even sweat) and the three strokes of the sword. I shall be reminded, I know, of the three leaps of the head of St Paul in Rome after decapitation; but humor, divine or human, was certainly involved in that phenomenon too. I am not sure that Virginia's somewhat compulsory adherence to chastity was not what stirred the Wife of Bath to inspiration for her long preamble (if the traditional Group D may follow C). Yet such observations as these must not be exaggerated to the point of saying that the poet laughed at the predicament and martyrdom of Cecilia, or even at her power to survive the various torments to which she was subjected, or that he was amused by Virginia or the little Clerk or the rest. It is a matter of his personal temperament, even perhaps his psychology. As he noted the excessively early tendency of St Nicholas to asceticism (because, it seems, the Saint as a babe sucked only once on Wednesdays and Fridays or fast days), so where this delicate quality of humor was present he would temperamentally be moved to take notice, his interest was drawn, and his memory stored the point or the plot for future use. Where we have the combination of high seriousness and humor, as in the little Clerk and his song, the result, I maintain, is sublime.

It is by such alchemy that Chaucer gains the amazing variety in his humor. Griselda's patience set in the midst of the controversy of the Wife of Bath is transmuted into something neither comic nor pathetic. Rich and strange in its effect on us, every stroke of the submission of Griselda recalls its inevitable effect upon the Wife of Bath. The more Griselda has to take, the more we recall what the Wife looks like when these things are being described, her face purple with rage and the air round her filled with the aroma of her blasphemies. For the Clerk by filling the canvas with Griselda's patience passes on the blows to the furious Wife. If Griselda is pathetic, through the pathos we see the red glare of the Wife's temper. And not far off is the rage of the Merchant, deceived by a young wife; shortly after, he gives us his story which so fatally turns its irony on the old husband rather than on the unfaithful May. Chaucer's range of power, his variety in the use of what might be taken as one stop in the instrument of expression, is boundless. We may recall the high spirits of the *Tale of Sir Thopas*, where humor has a form of appeal vastly different from that in the Marriage Cycle, or again the *Knight's Tale* with its humor of youth, or the *Nun's Priest's Tale* with the elegance of Chantecler, or the Monk's sentimentality and his conflict with the Host.

Range of appeal also in the social types which the poet has elected to describe has often been commented on. Critics have urged that he has brought the whole fourteenth century into his picture. The fact that some omissions occur and have been noted is only a further tribute in a way to his inclusiveness where it is still found. That the poet does little with the pastoral scene and the peasant doubtless reveals his urban interests quite as much as it does the limited preoccupation the whole Middle Ages showed with reference to the bucolic. Their poets in general did not go about looking for a presence in nature that disturbed them with joy. Nor is there any pantheism in Chaucer's outlook. Except for the vigor of his enjoyment of nature, and his keen sense of the delicious things that happen out of doors — the "shoures soote," the unfolding of flowers, the softest of breezes blowing — which convey an almost supernatural lustre to his descriptions, one might almost say that the details in his landscapes were all drawn from literary sources or manuscript illuminations. Here as in his plots the poet takes material gathered as a rule by others and lends it a characteristic intensification of value. What of his village scenes and village types? He does not give us much. But even here, as Mr. Coulton observes, "That the life of the mediaeval village had a true dignity at its best, and even a true glory in the highest sense of that word, no man can doubt who reads Chaucer's brief description of the Ploughman."

But granting the representative quality of the pilgrims, as far as social level and occupation is concerned, and noting also — as one may forget to do — the way in which the tales they tell add still other types and interests, the poet's interest shows still another kind of breadth: his knowledge of the young, the mature, and the old, of men as men and of women as women. The babe in the *Man of Law's Tale* and the little clerk described by the Prioress show little more than tenderness of portrayal; perhaps the Lawyer and the nun were not closely acquainted with children, and I could wish that the clergeoun showed a natural touch of boyish deviltry. If his song in the Jewish quarter had only been meant to flout the Jews the story would have been less saintly and more human.

> Morning, evening, noon and night,
> "Praise God!" sang Theocrite.

Chaucer's interest seems to begin, not with childhood but, with young men and young women when they show more that relates to character and its problems.

There can be no doubt that he is greatly attracted by youth. That is clear over and over again in the *Troilus*, and also in the *Knight's Tale* from the moment when Palamon and Arcite are found among the heap of the slain, both with the same coat of arms and richly clad. These two first emerged, I believe, in the twins of the *Thebaid* and the *Roman de Thèbes*; Boccaccio found and revivified them giving them a love story. In retelling part of the *Teseide* the English poet went quickly over the preliminary wars, and passed by all the opportunity for the satire of the Amazons to give his attention to the desperate young lovers. He might have done much with that delightful scene where the emancipated women are married to the Greeks under compulsion and vow not to return to their former folly, which includes, let us remember, the murder of their husbands:

> Nella prima follia non tornerieno,
> E che lor cari sempre mai avrieno.
> i, st. 135.

I am moved by the wish to ponder over material available to the poet which he did not use, such as, I believe, certain stories in the *Confessio Amantis* of Gower and in the *Romance of the Seven Sages*, perhaps even in the *Decameron*. But I cannot pause here for this digression. In any case Chaucer turned instead to the ironies of youth, and followed Arcite even to the death which if poignant is not lugubrious. Humor runs almost all the way through the tale without excepting the obsequies:

> "Why woldestow be deed," thise wommen crye,
> "And haddest gold ynough, and Emelye?"
>   A. 2835–2836.

Not far removed is this from "Up roos the sonne, and up roos Emelye" (A. 2273) or from "Yet song the larke, and Palamon also" (A. 2212). If this be levity, make the most of it; it is not destructive satire, but rather like the amused tolerance of Theseus who watches the battle in the woods when the lady is unaware of the existence of her suitors, and who has himself known love. Chaucer likes his young people. He likes the Squire of the pilgrimage, gives him at least the beginning of a good story, and suggests his praise in the words of the admiring Franklin. I think he likes the Canon's Yeoman, especially when he is belching out all the terms of his trade in a general muddle. And he even seems to like that rascal of the *Miller's Tale*, "hende Nicholas," for his very impudence.

He does not present his young ladies quite so flatteringly. Emelye's prayer to Diana, which might have been revealing, is devoid of personality except that it is pretty. The scene where she has to shift her allegiance from Arcite to Palamon, one that might have been filled with dramatic

effect or even a touch of irony, is empty so far as she is concerned. The virtuous ladies, I am afraid, are conventional or
vague in these stories on the way to Canterbury. The portrait of Virginia in the *Physician's Tale* begins with the favors
bestowed by Dame Nature; as in the case of Emelye her
color vies with that of the rose and the lily, or something of
the sort:

> And if that excellent was hire beautee,
> A thousand foold moore vertuous was she.
> In hire ne lakked no condicioun
> That is to preyse, as by discrecioun,
> As wel in goost as body chast was she;
> For which she floured in virginitee
> With alle humylitee and abstinence. . . .
>
> C. 39 ff.

"Sownynge in vertu" was her speech; in conduct she might
have been the Parson, in speech the Clerk, in morality and
abstinence a veritable Sir Thopas. There is one potentially
individualizing touch: she feigned sickness from time to
time to escape going to parties where there was likely to be
nonsense. But even this point of diplomacy seems to be
credited to her upright nature. Let no one suppose, however,
that I am here paying flippant tribute to vice by urging that
a little badness is necessary to add the tang of humanity to
characters in fiction. That is true of course — as far as it goes,
and it has been sentimentally celebrated with knowing looks,
the pose of the worldly wise, references to Wordsworth's
French daughter, and remarks with reference to the one
touch of nature that makes the whole world kin. But the
fact is, the counterpart is also true. One cannot have char-

acters made up of nothing but evil, or again they seem conventionally villainous and unreal. They must have just a bit of virtue, some redeeming feature to show their escape from simplicity. Jane Austen once had some fun planning an impossible book, "to open with father and daughter conversing in long speeches, elegant language, and a tone of high serious sentiment." She continues: "All the good will be unexceptionable in every respect. There will be no foibles or wickednesses but with the wicked, who will be completely depraved and infamous, hardly a resemblance of humanity left in them." The fact is, we must have a mixture in fiction as in life. This point is clear enough with Criseyde and the Wife of Bath, of whom much good may be said, although they do not belong in the category of noble, virtuous women.

It may be, however, tested in the marvelous account of the young wife in the *Miller's Tale*.

> Fair was this yonge wyf, and therwithal
> As any wezele hir body gent and smal.
>   A. 3233 ff.

I should like to quote it all, her fine get-up, her "likerous yë," her mouth as sweet as a stock of apples in the hay, her straight figure. As "blisful" she was to look at as is the early-ripe pear tree — in full bloom, I understand. Her coquetry with the thrifty-fingered Nicholas continues the picture, which goes on through the whole story. The vitality of the composition which has dictated such originality in figure of speech and other detail seems to tell the poet's own zest. He had no doubt a normal response to a woman's lure.

Alisoun's virtue consists mostly, I fear, in her beauty and agility. Chaucer saw her as a delicious morsel; she made him think of the loveliness of the early-pear tree, the fragrance of apples lying in hay, the softness of the wool of a wether. Constance and Griselda did not do all this. Such symbolism is not common in poetry anyhow until later writers sing cherry ripe of their ladies' lips. The best we can say for Alisoun is that she makes Nicholas work for what he gets. But Chaucer saw her as a fine product of nature, and any touch of perfection moved him; just so he might have described the pear tree itself or the ripe apple.

For such beauty one turns to Criseyde, who, in spite of the poet's affection and the admiration of everybody, is not wholly admirable. Although she is tender hearted, in some ways she is as hard as nails; her fearfulness is for herself, and she always has an eye to her own advantage. She is not so brisk as Alisoun; nor is she so sure of herself or centered with Griselda's unfailing stability. But if she is "slydynge of corage," she has the saving grace of her kindly attitude toward Pandarus and of her love for Troilus. Chaucer does better with such a type than with the preponderantly virtuous. Prudence in the story of Melibeus and Madame Pertelote have some reality but we do not know much about them. Why did he deal chiefly or most convincingly with ladies marked with Cressid's weakness — Alisoun, May, the Merchant's wife, perhaps the Host's wife, Phebus's wife, and the Wife of Bath, as contrasted with Emelye, Constance, Griselda, Dorigen, Cecilia, and the Prioress? It would seem that in life he had not found a blessed Beatrice to lead him upward to enlightenment. Among his gods and goddesses it is Venus who thwarts Arcite (who after all won the tournament) and Proserpine who successfully defends May. He can write of virtuous men, however — the Clerk, the Parson, the Franklin, the Knight, the Man of Law, the Physician, and apparently the Host; Theseus, Arviragus, perhaps Virginius, in the stories, and plenty more. The Host, Harry Bailey, is quite as substantial as the Wife of Bath.

I have already said that the most contemptible rogues are among the men. Chaucer enjoyed the company of most of them and liked them. But, be it noted, there is no trace of evidence that he was unaware of their rascality or obliterated it. His moral sense was not paralyzed by his affections. He wrote much about morality, and indeed it is hard to-day to understand why he spent so much time on the *Melibeus* or the *Parson's Tale*. Moral passages are strewn in his works; and the modern critic calls them edifying or medieval examples of the sententious, and passes them by. But in his own day and for some time after the poet was praised for his moral doctrine. Lydgate and Hoccleve use terms that show they regarded him as an improving influence — as if that would be generally taken as a point in his favor. Yet his poetry is not doctrinaire, and it must be insisted that he does not view human nature primarily from the moral angle. While the basis for human action is moral, Chaucer sees his characters as beings with passions and tastes and weaknesses and aspirations, all of which enormously draw his interest and stir his imagination. He is vastly interested in life. The social or spiritual utility of these gifts of nature is a later consideration. He likes his people, good or bad (all but the Pardoner); his was not a temperament to draw up a universal cosmography and place his characters therein according to an Aristotelian or Christian scale of values. His pilgrims perform the task of judging one another for themselves. It is true, nevertheless, that humor requires some judgment. Think how Jane Austen (let alone Thackeray or Swift) sharpens her pen! Even Dickens raises at times a harsh tribunal. Chaucer knew what morality was, and in the last analysis he did not escape the obligation to reveal its issues. For if art is real, the artist like the prophet must include moral observations.

Lowell's comment is ingenious but misleading when he remarks: "With Dante the main question is the saving of the soul, with Chaucer it is the conduct of life. The distance between them is almost that between holiness and prudence." It is the mystical element in Dante, I think, that is responsible for this idea. With both writers the main question is the conduct of life in the proper fashion for the saving of the soul. Aside from poetic gifts and profundity of nature, the contrast is rather to be found in the fact that Dante's gaze in following the divine comedy is fixed on the goal, Chaucer's is fixed on the creatures engaged in the process. In other words the chief interest with the English poet is human nature. There is much talk about love in Dante, but sometimes it seems more theoretical than real, as if it were described scientifically with a graph plotting its location in the universe. Chaucer loves human beings. The *Divine Comedy* is in a real sense a last judgment; Chaucer's works represent a drama in the course of its action, in which there is vast significance long before its fulfilment. To come to the end may mean (despite the proverb) that in understanding all things we shall be less forgiving, and the tolerance implied in humor will evaporate. But while we poor beasts are still in ignorance of most of the great secrets, perhaps we can laugh more readily and feel less compunction, because no final judgment is involved. To put it another way Chaucer seems more light-hearted than Dante, because in displaying his characters he knows most of them have another chance. There is little room for the whimsical or tentative in the *Inferno* or the *Paradiso*. But much jesting is possible on the road to Canterbury.

Chapter VII

CHAUCER AND THE COMMON PEOPLE

AFTER the long strife for the emancipation of poetry in the modern period, one demand, curiously enough, in our own day seems to be that poets shall be moral, and even, on occasion, didactic, or suffer the penalty of hostile criticism. A modern poet must preach communism or fascism, or show a social consciousness, or proclaim the virtues of the proletariat, or attack the politicians of his day, unless he wants to be told that he lives in an ivory tower. For all the humanism in his verse Geoffrey Chaucer has not escaped his share of this criticism, apparently because he did not spend much time preaching humanitarianism. The sufferings of the English poor were great, it is certainly true, in the latter half of the fourteenth century; Jusserand once observed that "a multitude of causes, among which the Great Plague of 1349 ranks as the chief, had . . . overturned the relations of the working classes with the rich, and the proportions between the value of wages and that of the objects necessary to life. In face of a need of emancipation which arose on all sides, parliament . . . passed hard laws which prescribed the maintenance of the *statu quo ante pestem*." Gower and Hoccleve felt the gloom of this unhappy time, when, as Professor Coulton with less felicity than usual remarks, ". . . there hung always over men's lives the shadow of God's hand — or rather, as they too often felt, of Satan's." "Where Langland cries aloud in anger, threatening the world with hell-fire, Chaucer looks on and smiles," protests Mr. Aldous Huxley, and precisely in the same vein Mr. Coulton objects that "Where Gower sees an England more hopelessly given over to the Devil than even in Carlyle's most dyspeptic nightmares — where the robuster Langland sees an impending religious Armageddon . . . there Chaucer, with incurable optimism, sees chiefly a Merry England. . . ."

The purpose of this chapter is to inquire whether this interesting charge is after all justified. Is it true that Chaucer saw the horrors of his day and was untouched by them, that he had access to Court for purposes of complaint and remained merely the polite entertainer? A brief survey of even medieval romance, where we find portraits of Grim and the cook in *Havelok*, the hero of *Fergus*, various realistic hags and merciful executioners, the butcher in *Octovian*, seamen, pilgrims, and beggars, not to speak of the material in fabliaux and satires and indeed in Chaucer's own sources, makes it necessary to moderate the old statement that the poet introduced the lower classes to literature. He hardly appears democratic in his handling of the mob in the *Clerk's Tale* and the *Troilus*. Like Swift did he feel affection for Hubert and Harry and Nicolas, but not so much for the "stormy peple, unsad and evere untrewe," disliking the rabblement perhaps as they "shouted and clapped their chopped hands"? In the *Nun's Priest's Tale* and in the *Troilus* his allusions to Jack Straw and his "meynee," and, for that matter, that in the *Pardoner's Tale* to the Plague, are only those of a spectator. Even his Friar refused to deal with any but rich folk; and, despite the pretence that social station would be set aside in the story-telling on the pilgrimage, the Knight after all led off at least for the sake of decorum. Anyone who seeks the reformer in Chaucer, and with puritan zeal disdains the man of the world, may be tempted on these terms to set him down once and for all as a cynic.

But, in any fair review of the situation, we are bound to observe at the start that the poet's opportunities at Court for suggesting measures of social reform were drastically limited. Only too readily could his audience turn away, or bid him choose another tale — as the pilgrims silenced the Monk. Yet considering the chief interest of the polite litera-ture of his day, it is remarkable, after all, what democratic sympathy Chaucer shows — how little he has confined his material to people of high station, and what a wealth of knowledge he has of the lower classes. The millers, reeves, summoners, cooks, perhaps the Canon's Yeoman, the guilds-men and their wives, not only on the pilgrimage but in the tales themselves, how sharp a contrast they make with the characters and preoccupations of romance and Court of Love literature! After Chaucer's early period he somehow happened to choose a large number of stories of humble life, and certainly he introduced at least the fabliau to respectable literary circles. Although Mr. Coulton dismisses the cottage woman of the *Nun's Priest's Tale* pretty much as a lay figure, the mother of the little Clergeoun in the *Prioress's Tale* is also a "povre wydwe," and the pathos of the story consists partly in the simplicity of the background — however traditional. In the *Clerk's Tale* the reason why serious people condemned the applause of the mob (a passage added by Chaucer) was partly because the crowd was glad that the Marquis had taken a lady of higher lineage. This then is not really "aristocratic contempt for the multitude," and Mr. Coulton admits that ". . . all that is most touching in that tale turns on the peasant's patience under injustice. . . ."

Chaucer, however, is more outspoken in the *Parson's Tale*. Here pride in riches and lineage is again vigorously denounced, and here is the radical doctrine (borrowed no doubt, but that does not affect the case) that "of swich seed as cherles spryngen, of swich seed spryngen lordes. As wel may the cherl be saved as the lord. . . . I rede thee, certes, that thou, lord, werke in swich wise with thy cherles that they rather love thee than drede. I woot wel ther is degree above degree, as reson is; and skile is that men do hir devoir ther as it is due; but certes, extorcions and despit of youre underlynges is dampnable" (I. 761 ff.). This is not love of the individual and contempt for the crowd; in this light the whole section on Avarice in the Tale deserves to be re-read, especially such a sentence as "Thus may ye seen that the gilt disserveth thraldom, but nat nature" — not unlike Rousseau's more sentimental dictum that man is born free but everywhere we find him in chains. "Humble folk been Cristes freendes," is as fairly characteristic of Chaucer as any other quotation from his works; and need we add that the portrait of his Friar who consulted only the rich was touched with satire? But some critics will regard all this material in the *Parson's Tale* as only perfunctory. We have learned, however, that with all its light-hearted setting even the *Tale of Melibeus* can hardly be set aside in that way. After all, the tedious work of translating such a document means something in the poet's interest; and here especially in the tale which concludes the series it is very doubtful whether the writer offers us nothing more than an edifying and insincere performance intended as a sop to the "sad" and a pose for the orthodox. Small wonder if the poet appear like a cynic if we regard him as insincere whenever he is moral.

But we have evidence that in this case at least he meant exactly what he said. We find, in fact, that he has gone out of his way in his verse to give expression to the same ideas in passages which can hardly be quite justified in terms of the plot. In the *Wife of Bath's Tale*, in the long harangue on gentilesse, he has taken from others a discussion of the problem wherein we are told that God wills "that of hym we clayme oure gentilesse" (D. 1129–1130). In his moral ballade on the same subject he says:

> For unto vertu longeth dignitee,
> And nought the revers, saufly dar I deme,
> Al were he mytre, croune, or diademe.
> *Gentilesse*, 5–7.

A man's a man for a' that! Similar ideas appear in the *Former Age*.

More remarkable still, perhaps, is the well-known passage against tyrants which is introduced, not into a sermon or metrical homily, but into a Court of Love poem, the prologue of the *Legend of Good Women*, apparently for the sole reason that this work was to be sent to the royal palace. Here the king is asked to have compassion on poor folk, and the passage is rendered more emphatic in the later form of the Prologue. Perhaps the occasion of this reference was the Pontefract episode of John of Gaunt, or possibly it had to do with the first petition to Parliament; in any case, the appeal for both rich and poor is here. Professor Samuel Moore remarked: "We ought to recognize . . . that the matter is certainly over-emphasized, if Chaucer was concerned exclusively with the God of Love and not at all with King Richard. Alceste's speech is nearly one-fifth of the B Prologue, and more than a fifth of A." Again, the same doctrine is voiced in *Lak of Stedfastnesse* asking the King to cherish his folk and hate extortion.

For his social theories, as in so many other matters, Chaucer found guidance in Boethius. Here was the material for *Gentilesse* and the *Former Age* and much on the subject of good and fair government. Here in his own translation he uses a phrase that seems to have passed unnoticed, a phrase with a history: "Whan it was in the sowre hungry tyme, ther was establissed or cryed grevous and unplitable coempcioun, that men sayen wel it schulde gretly tormenten and endamagen al the provynce of Campayne, I took stryf ayens the provost of the pretorie for comune profit" (*Boece*, I, pr. 4, ll. 93 ff.). The "comune profit"! It corresponds to "communis commodi ratione" in the original, but the English words are found elsewhere. The phrase occurs twice in the B-text of *Piers Plowman*, where the mice and rats meet in conference and plan to bell the cat for their "common profit." Gower uses it in the *Confessio Amantis* in a Miltonic passage attacking Church controversy. It is found many times in this period; and, as the instances cited by Miss Temple and Miss Everett show, it appears in manuscripts which deal with social questions, especially those discussing the duties of the perfect prince. Miss Allen is frank to call it a "favourite phrase of fourteenth-century Socialism, both in England and in France."

Chaucer uses it several times again, in the *Parliament* and in the *Clerk's Tale*. In the latter Griselda fulfils the perfect duty of the marchioness:

> The commune profit koude she redresse.
> Ther nas discord, rancour, ne hevynesse
> In al that land, that she ne koude apese,
> And wisely brynge hem alle in reste and ese.
>
> E. 431 ff.

It seems to have a special connotation as one observes the recurrence of the phrase here and there — like such modern expressions as "public ownership," "starvation wage," and "communism." Taking the use of this phrase together with other passages of similar import, the total evidence of Chaucer's concern for the oppressed is considerable, to say the least. His words are few, but he speaks out more than once, and indeed more than twice, with a trenchant power that a less good-natured writer would hardly command. It is quite possible that for direct action in high places he had more success than Langland or Gower. In any case, it is clear what results he wanted, and what reforms engaged his ardor. But the use of such words must not be taken to imply that the poet was primarily bent on social reform, any more than it was Wycliffe's vocation to be entertaining. What Chaucer meant by his use of "common profit" may be guessed from a passage in the *Parson's Tale*, from the same discussion on Avarice as that from which I have quoted above: ". . . but for as muche as the estaat of hooly chirche ne myghte nat han be, ne the commune profit myghte nat han be kept, ne pees and rest in erthe, but if God hadde ordeyned that som men hadde hyer degree and som men lower, therfore was sovereyntee ordeyned, to kepe and mayntene and deffenden hire underlynges or hire subgetz in resoun, as ferforth as it lith in hire power, and nat to destroyen hem ne confounde" (I. 772–773). Evidently he was not an extreme radical. If he had a sympathetic interest in the Lollard movement, it was apparently not for its heresy but for its moral sincerity and fervor. That is the theme that harmonizes his description of the Parson with the *Parson's Tale*. What the poet's own charities were, we are not likely to know; perhaps first he wrought and afterward he taught. Our critics have finally to deal with Chaucer's description of the Plowman, as sweet at heart as his brother the Parson. Here is a suggestion that the simplicity we enjoy in the account of Griselda and the little Clergeoun is native to the poet himself and not merely taken over from his sources. The Plowman had driven many a load of manure; he was an honest and a good laborer; he loved God best with all his whole heart, and did his job, paid his tithes, and didn't kick much. Idealistically or not, the Plowman is meant to be a type, representing a whole group: in his stout figure he includes the whole class of decent laboring-men.

Chaucer's optimism consists in stressing the positive, more than in denying the negative, but his didacticism is none the less real for all that. He spreads the contagious propaganda of a kindly view of human nature. In the fourteenth century it is noteworthy that he extends this kindly view to the lower classes, even when he is talking with kings; and his influence inevitably would tend to create a broader social sympathy. Gower and Langland give all the necessary evidence that they pitied the poor. Chaucer without sentimentality appears to have loved them.

Chapter VIII

CHAUCER AND MEDIEVAL
ROMANCE

CHIVALRY, we are told, received its deathblow from
the rise of the merchant class — a theory which seems
to rest on the popular notion that industrialism is always to
be blamed for a collapse of ideals. Some historians, however,
point out that chivalry waned contemporaneously with the
Crusades. Still others recall the fact that in warfare the
knight became impractical when the unmounted yeoman
grew in prestige. Many are the causes that lead to changes of
this kind. Whatever may be the truth in this case, it is safe
to say that when Chaucer was alive and hale fully one hundred and fifty years had passed since the time when men
rescued fair ladies from famished dragons. To Chrétien de
Troyes and other minstrels of his period there was doubtless an element of stout realism in the recovery of Guinivere,
or in the quest of the Grail. The twelfth century still had the
lure of the Holy Land to draw its fervor, and the magic of
the Far East to make it believe that nothing is but what is
not. Through the numberless romances the knights became
familiar figures; and the very quantity of romantic literature tended to reduce the quantity, if not the quality, of romance. Realism becomes difficult with distance, however,
and in the fourteenth century it was rather to the imagination which found special glamor in the remote or impossible

that these stories offered an appeal. Perhaps this is another instance of an old idealism becoming transmuted into poetry, the religion of chivalry giving place to its mythology.

Without question there were some excellent stories written under the impulse of the alliterative revival, but these seem to have been mostly translations or revisions of old material. To "olde bokes" one had to go for the original, — "as men may in thise olde gestes rede," — for in Chaucer's day Gawain "with his olde curtesye" has gone forever to fairye, and Lancelot, who knew so well of "subtil lookyng and dissymulynges" and all the form of courtliness, he, alas! is dead! With the romances of the twelfth and thirteenth centuries the case is somewhat different. Occasionally, it is true, an author strives to give the impression that he has found his source in some ancient manuscript; for what writer in the Middle Ages did not prefer to call up authorities from the vasty deep, if possible? But, often as not, the beginnings are abrupt, with no apology except that the tale is a good one.

Considering the multitude of romances in the earlier period, then, it seems likely that one reason for the number of competent or artistic productions in the late fourteenth century, including the Constance group and *Syr Gawayn and the Grene Knyght*, which show a power that depends on more than a survival of interest, is that they already offered the charm of the antique. The use of alliteration seems to support this idea. In relation to the whole field, therefore, Chaucer is in a position similar to that of Malory and Spenser.

From this point of view it is worth fresh inquiry to dis-

cover what is Chaucer's response to the thoroughly romantic appeal of this subject matter, which any well-read man
of his day could hardly escape knowing pretty extensively.
The term "romantic" in such a connection deserves an explanation, perhaps, and yet it seems natural and fitting for
the word to mean "whatever has to do with romances." In
that sense the implications are, for a while at least, clear, and
thus it may stand for the course of this discussion. To what
extent does the romantic quality (or the quality of the romances) appear in Chaucer's work? By glancing over the
five hundred years of criticism and allusion which Miss
Spurgeon has collected for us, one may learn from various
angles the nature of Chaucer's realism; and it is essential to
continue to enrich our interpretation of this side of his nature. But what is he as a romanticist? Is he so steadily the
realist that he never lives in Arcady? By his time the oaks
were old in Sherwood Forest and probably in Arden too!

As a matter of fact, a critic in a scientific age may become
almost depressed in spirit when he observes the quantity of
Chaucer's poetry which, in some way or another, seems to
belong to the category of romance. This is no realist, whose
reading was so one-sided. Even his speech echoes the romantic language. A collection of interesting examples has
been made, and here may be found such figures as: "ful lyk
a fiers leoun," "as freshe as is the brighte someres day,"
"freshe as faucon comen out of muwe," "whyt as foom" —
figures that the casual reader might think were taken from
a fine observation of real life, which a realist's inquiring eye
could make. Furthermore, in all his works there are allusions
to romantic material. The *Book of the Duchess* refers to the

cycles of Troy, Alexander, and Charlemagne, and includes
an entirely unnecessary borrowing from *Octovian Imperator*.
The poem called *Against Women Unconstant* brings in Can-
dace and Criseyde. The *House of Fame*, packed with proper-
ties from the romantic storehouse, adds Arthurian sources
in the allusions to English Geoffrey and to Isolde. The *Parliament of Fowls, Anelida and Arcite*, and the *Knight's Tale* owe
a substantial debt to the Cycle of Thebes. The *Troilus* calls
up Troy for the space of a love affair. The *Legend of Good
Women* gives us Trojan material. The *Man of Law's Tale*
belongs to the Constance group. The *Monk's Tale* presents
the story of Alexander. The *Nun's Priest's Tale* alludes to
Lancelot and Ganilon. *Sir Thopas* is a parody of romance.
The *Wife of Bath's Tale* gives us the Loathly Lady; the
Clerk's Tale belongs to the Griselda cycle and the *Lai le
Freine* group; the *Squire's Tale* is of true romance all com-
pact — as far as it goes; the *Merchant's Tale* alludes to the
"paradys terrestre," to Wade's boat, and to Pluto, King of
Fairye, who, the footnotes tell us, comes from *Sir Orpheo*;
the *Franklin's Tale* is a lay, and the *Manciple's Tale* might just
as well be as not.

Such a summary as this is pardonable in view of the total
effect, to recall with some vividness the pertinent fact that
subject matter which in some way or other is related to
romance is widely used in Chaucer's works. One might go
further and observe that romance-reading in a book was
as characteristic of Chaucer's maturity as of his youth, and
that, if frequency of allusion counts for anything, the matter
of Troy appears most largely. We might go on to add that,
except for an occasional moral lapse into the didactic or

pious, Chaucer never quite got away from the spell of the romantic; that the realistic forms of literature, such as the satires or *débats*, do not seem to have caught his interest much, unless you bother with the fabliaux, which, being human, he could hardly avoid.

But most of these inferences, and, indeed, much of this material, vanish on closer examination.

> . . . He clapte his handes two,
> And farewel! al oure revel was ago.
> F. 1203–1204.

In all the works many of the allusions come second-hand from the *Roman de la Rose*. Many of the similes and metaphors which are found in general use in Chaucer and in the romances were probably also current in the ordinary speech of the day ("whyt as foom" depends neither on romantic imagination nor acute powers of observation). Or, in some cases, the stories come from works which are anything but romantic in nature. Thus Chaucer may have taken his material on Alexander partly from Quintus Curtius or from the tale in the *Gesta Romanorum*; and that on Constance from the Anglo-Norman Chronicle and Gower; that on Griselda from Petrarch's treatise. Even references like that to Octovyen in the *Book of the Duchess*, and that to Pluto, King of Fairye, in the *Merchant's Tale*, are of dubious origin. Perhaps Octovyen is brought in, not by way of romance at all, but as the emperor of the Golden Age, which, the poet thus implies, obtained during the happy reign of Edward the Third. It is similarly that Deschamps several times refers to him. "Quant verray je le temps Octovien," he asks,

"Que toute paix fut au monde affermée?" And, as it happens, Pluto is mentioned neither in *Sir Orpheo* nor in *King Orfeo* as the King of Fairye, but as an ancestor of Orpheo's father. Even in the *Troilus*, when the ladies are listening to the "Sege of Thebes" (an episode which is not in the *Filostrato*), what they hear is apparently the "geste" of Statius, and not a romance at all.

So one might continue. The mention of a "romaunce" in the *Book of the Duchess* may refer to Ovid, or more likely to the *Dit de la Fonteinne Amoureuse*. One scholar has suggested that the poet seems to have taken prose romances rather lightly. After thoroughly going over the whole ground of Chaucer's "learning," Miss Hammond made an even more extreme statement. "Were it not for the full knowledge of the English metrical romances displayed in the Rime of Sir Thopas," she remarks, "we might have assumed that Chaucer had done no reading in that field, and had picked up the allusions to Gawain as courteous, Tristram and Lancelot as typical lovers, and Arthur's court as the centre of chivalry, from the literary commonplace of his time."

But surely exception should be made for the works which borrow most liberally from documents of this kind — namely, in the case of the *Troilus* from the *Filostrato* and the *Knight's Tale* from the *Teseide*! Long ago, however, with an acumen which has been common property ever since, Professor Ker observed that "Chaucer's *Troilus and Criseyde* is the poem in which medieval romance passes out of itself into the form of the modern novel." If he found his plot in a romance, therefore (although I am not sure that the *Filostrato*, if "graceful," is quite so "superficial" as Mr. Ker

seems to imply), he straightway changed the tone and quality of his story and produced something else. Professor Karl
Young has argued to different effect, and has tried to put the
Troilus back into the romantic category once more. His
study is useful in so far as it makes clear the features in
which Chaucer has intensified the romantic values of the
poem. But a classification to be illuminating, I think, must reveal more than that. Chaucer has intensified *all* the values of
the poem. The ways in which it differs significantly from its
source have to do with its philosophy and with its realistic
treatment of character. Granting that some romances show
a fair degree of characterization, we must observe that when
they do they approach the novel, and that in this respect
Chaucer's poem leads them all, leaving far behind the world
of mere glamor and supernaturalistic thrills. Or no, I am
mistaken! — it is a tragedy, is it not, in which the youthful
characters introduce the saving presence of humor? What
then of the *Teseide* and Chaucer's transformation of that
poem for the purposes of his Knight? This Italian *magnum
opus*, which, according to Mr. Ker, is "the first of the solemn
row of modern epics," becomes, he thought, "a complete
and perfect version of a medieval romance, worked out with
all the resources of Chaucer's literary study and reflexion...."
Here, we may suppose, is his most nearly perfect expression
of the romantic spirit.

But when we stop to think of the nature of true romance,
as it has endeared itself to readers, and obtained a permanency
in literature as' a special type, does this observation seem
quite satisfactory? At first sight it is more plausible, I believe,
than Mr. Young's similar comment on the *Troilus*. But let us

remember the obvious fact that for critical purposes at least it is hardly profitable to classify as romance every sort of literary production in the Middle Ages which will not fit in with the religious, didactic, dramatic, or satiric writings. Nor is the proper criterion to be based on such treatments of subject matter as the use of adventure or the emphasis on love; for while romance persists in later periods in a duly recognizable form, adventure and love are found useful, not only here but elsewhere, among realists and even allegorists. The characteristic which marks romance, I think, and defines its quality is rather a primary appeal, through the nature or the manipulation of the subject matter, to the imagination. "Romance means nothing, if it does not convey some notion of mystery and fantasy," said Mr. Ker.

Remote or mysterious or fanciful the stuff of which it is made may be, or again, the things it presents may not be so very far off or unhappy, nor the battles those of so very long ago; but in either case the imagination is touched, follows readily, and comprehends, while one's reason is mystified or held in abeyance. The use of creatures only to be seen at twilight, a special absence of explanations, a departure from that air of verisimilitude where the reader is tempted to check up the veracity of the author, these traits are what we delight in when we read the stories of the French Vulgate, or the late and essentially romantic stories of Charlemagne, or such tales as the *Awntyrs of Arthure at the Terne Wathelyn*. Not that realism is never used; but that when it is, romance, for the while, is less evident. When the table of food appears without even a wicked steward to account for it, or when Parsifal fails to ask the question which will relieve the stricken king — then, call it the mood of wonder, if you like, the artistic satisfaction comes by way of the imagination. This, let it be understood, is no attempt to define the meaning of nineteenth-century romanticism, which introduces enough and differently baffling problems of its own. This refers rather to what is strictly within the fold of medieval romance, and perhaps it is only another way of indicating what one critic has called the "incredible" nature of the material.

Whatever be the terms used to describe it, the quality itself is clear, I think, and this quality hardly predominates in the *Knight's Tale*. Mr. Ker had in mind, obviously, the historical rather than a critical use of the word "romance," and, on that ground, his dictum is valid. Yet in *Epic and Romance*, where the discussion in question occurs, his task is mainly to give a critical meaning to this expression, and so he challenges fresh criticism with the effort.

In revising Boccaccio's story it does not appear that Chaucer made any changes in the general direction of what we have described as romantic. Among other modifications he quite deliberately introduced the following important ones: First, the long warfare at the beginning is omitted, and the emphasis falls at once on the relationship of the three characters — Palamon, Arcite, and Emelye. Secondly, the element of chance, often so vital to romantic literature, is diminished by the development in some respects of what Mr. Ker called the "classical panoply." Thirdly, the irony of the story, based in part on the parallelism of the two lovers, is greatly magnified in importance, and, by the omission of Arcite's long complaint and the substitution for it of his speech, "Allas, why pleynen folk so in commune" (A. 1251 ff.), the sentimentality of the original is much reduced.

In regard to the second of these points, one cannot fail to observe the humor which is included when Saturn is called upon to settle the controversy between Venus and Mars. It seems, these deities have too promptly answered the prayers addressed to them, without consultation as to the merits of those who have prayed. As to Dame Fortune, although she is constantly blamed in Boccaccio for the action of the tragedy, Chaucer tends to ignore her and adds a passage from Boethius in which Destiny is described as the servant of God. Chaucer speaks of:

> The destinee, ministre general,
> That executeth in the world over al
> The purveiaunce that God hath seyn biforn. . . .
> A. 1663–1665.

This passage strengthens the plot at the moment of its greatest weakness, the moment when Theseus happens to come upon the two fighters. Instead of ascribing the coincidence to the workings of Fortune, Chaucer explains that it is only one of the strange episodes which Destiny has brought to pass, not through caprice, but as part of the Divine plan. Boccaccio refers elsewhere to "l'alta ministra del mondo Fortuna," and thus in the *Knight's Tale* we find a reminiscence of this line in the *Teseide* and also of Dante's "general ministra e duce" where Fortune herself is represented as God's handmaid. The control of Chaucer's story is, therefore, rational rather than casual, a point which may explain why the merits of the heroes are more nearly taken into account, and why Palamon rather than Arcite, as in the

Teseide, is the first to see Emelye (since the plot requires that he be the hero ultimately to win her). This does not obviate the condition that Arcite's fate is still something of a sentimental tragedy; but it is certainly true that the emphasis on this side of the story is lightened. Enjoyment of the characters outweighs paradoxically our concern for them. In the loss of Arcite we are not inconsolable for:

> ". . . certeinly a man hath moost honour
> To dyen in his excellence and flour. . . ."
>   A. 3047–3048.

Character is enriched in Chaucer's version even at the expense of the splendor of the tournament and the excitement of combat. Thus there is no intention here of creating a romance of chivalry, if in such literature passages at arms are of chief importance. Nor is the love affair stressed for its own sake so much as for the humor it reflects upon the heroes. With remarkably simple technique Chaucer's story gives us the irony of youth, the irony of young men in their tremendous concern for a young lady; and the opportunity for dramatic reflections of that kind is what, I think, originally commended the plot to the special interest of the English poet. In this quality and in the symmetrical structure the story closely resembles *Troilus and Criseyde*, to which it probably stands closest in time of composition.

Notice that hardly a moment is lost before we come to the two young knights lying "by and by" "bothe in oon armes" —

> Of whiche two Arcita highte that oon,
> And that oother knyght highte Palamon,
>   A. 1013–1014.

which gains in effect if you fall into a slight singsong as you read it. Both of them become pale "as asshen colde" under stress of their experiences within and without the prison wall; and of their retinue in the tournament we are told:

> So evene, withouten variacioun,
> Ther nere swiche compaignyes tweye . . .
> A. 2588–2589.

Their parallelism might be compared, without offense, to that of Rosencrantz and Guildenstern; and their battle — not to be profane — might evoke memories of Tweedle-dum and Tweedledee; but the very exaggeration involved in the comparison ruins its critical meaning and should not be tolerated — after it is once said. Besides, Chaucer has made the heroes so much alive, and we are so sympathetic with their desperate case, that any observation of their similarity is clumsy. Arcite is the more manly figure, a true knight; Palamon is steadfastly the lover, who is willing to turn state's evidence to win his game. "Palamon is much more passionate and jealous," remarked ten Brink, "much less magnanimous than the corresponding character in Boccaccio, and Arcite also becomes much more positive and violent in [Chaucer's] hands."

In many ways the humor of the poem turns on the characterization. There is nothing in the *Teseide* to match the intense youth of Palamon's speech to Theseus. "Slay me," he cries, but quickly adds,

> "Or sle hym first, for though thow knowest it lite,
> This is thy mortal foo, this is Arcite . . ."
> A. 1723–1724.

Nor is there anything to match the flavor of the sentimentalism into which Theseus falls in discoursing on his ancient loves:

> "A man moot ben a fool, or yong or oold, —
> I woot it by myself ful yore agon,
> For in my tyme a servant was I oon."
> A. 1812–1814.

This is a whole world different from "Ma perchè gia innamorato fui," which is pretty cold logic. Take the very speech already cited, in which Arcite bursts forth:

> "Allas, why pleynen folk so in commune
> On purveiaunce of God, or of Fortune . . ."
> A. 1251–1252.

While he thus complains that he is now out of prison (at a time when Palamon is lamenting that he himself has not been able to get free), Arcite is unaware that this is his first step in the process of actually obtaining a sight of Emelye. But the points of irony in the *Knight's Tale* have been often listed. It is hardly necessary to recall that one knight wins the tournament but fails to get the lady, while the other loses in the joust but gets her. Nor must I observe here that, although there is pathos in the death of Arcite, genuine as it is, even that receives a new touch in such a passage as the following:

> "Why woldestow be deed," thise wommen crye,
> "And haddest gold ynough, and Emelye?"
> A. 2835–2836.

(I realize that I have quoted these lines before; but I expect to quote them, in due course, many times.) We do not dwell too long on the funeral or follow Arcite's soul through the spheres as Boccaccio wanted us to. Nor need I mention the fact that Chaucer provides us with the "delicious Egeus," and also with the speech of his son, who seems to have something in his blood from "these tedious old fools." Nor must I add that in his description of the funeral pyre and the funeral, Chaucer uses that quite familiar formula of abbreviators — "I do not need to tell you," "I need not observe," "nor do I need to recall" — which serves so often as an underhanded device for setting forth old material, and that he then gives an interminable list of details of supposed solemnity:

> But how the fyr was maked up on highte,
> Ne eek the names that the trees highte,
> As ook, firre, birch, aspe, alder, holm, popler,
> Wylugh, elm, plane, assh, box, chasteyn, lynde, laurer,
> Mapul, thorn, bech, hasel, ew, whippeltree, —
> How they weren feld, shal nat be toold for me;
> Ne hou the goddes ronnen up and doun,
> Disherited of hire habitacioun,
> In whiche they woneden in reste and pees,
> Nymphes, fawnes, and amadrides; ·
> Ne hou the beestes and the briddes alle
> Fledden for fere, whan the wode was falle;
> Ne how the ground agast was of the light —
>
> A. 2919–2931.

and so on, for thirty lines and more.

One critic has observed the changes that the poet makes for the sake of realism, especially in the feudal elements of the story; and another has pointed out that in the garden scene we feel a clear impulse from the vernal wood. But obviously that is not all. It is the tone of something rather like levity which is most surprising in this tale. The Knight seems to have cared less for the mysterious and the uncanny than for some other things, and, above all, he has a sense of humor. With a sympathy the more wholesome for his grace, he gives us the tragedy of youth, by means of a characterization which is not over-individualized but sure.

All this bears directly on Mr. Ker's definitions. "The success of epic poetry," he said, "depends on the author's power of imagining and representing characters. . . . Without dramatic representation of the characters, epic is mere history or romance. . . ." "The history of the early heroic literature of the Teutonic tongues, and of the epics of old France, comes to an end in the victory of various romantic schools. . . . From within and without, from the resources of native mythology and superstition and from the fascination of Welsh and Arabian stories, there came the temptation to forget the study of character. . . ." These passages in their own context in *Epic and Romance* show that character is the main interest of the epic. But, while it would be absurd to argue that the *Knight's Tale* belongs to that type, the changes that Chaucer made in his material are certainly not pointed the other way.

On the other hand, I would not try to maintain that humor and dramatic irony are absent in the romances. We find good dramatic irony in that burly production, *Havelok*, where the hero and Goldborough are loathe to wed because they both think that Havelok's station is too low for such a union. In *King Horn* there is irony where Athulf longs for Horn's arrival — when as a matter of fact he is present all the time. The many recognition scenes in other poems involve in some cases the same implication. If the *Knight's Tale* must be a romance, I would say that it is after the manner of the English Cycle. Characterization too is not foreign to romance. One thinks of the tradition of Sir Kay and of Gawain, or of such figures as the butcher in *Octovian*. You can go even further, and say that not all of the known romances are purely romantic. But the distinguishing quality of this kind of literature, that expression of the imagination "that possesses" — Mr. Ker himself put it thus — "the mystery and the spell of everything remote and unattainable," is not what Chaucer contributed, any more than it is what he found in his source. One may question whether humor creates a healthy atmosphere for such a quality, and whether, if the *Knight's Tale* be classified as romance, such pigeonholing tells anything about the romantic temper in Chaucer.

Yet no one is likely to say, with Lowell, that in *Sir Thopas* Chaucer gives the *coup de grâce* to chivalry. The *Squire's Tale* is an answer to that. Unfinished as it is, and drawn, not from the traditional cycles but from Oriental material received, probably, at second hand, it shows a conscious effort at a sustained performance in the romantic vein, and it seems to have sprung from the poet's ripest years. Grant that the *Wife of Bath's Tale* is mainly satiric, and the *Franklin's Tale* domestic, and you still have a residue of isolated passages which show the same spirit.

Indeed it is possible to make out a good case for the theory that the *House of Fame* was written for the appeal of romantic adventure. This is not to say that no allegorical intention was implied, or that personal allusions were totally absent (or were to be in the finished product). But the wealth of material, borrowed for this poem from romantic sources, or related to interests of that kind, leads one to suspect that Chaucer meant to go beyond the machinery of the Court of Love; at least one can be sure that he was not content with that alone. In the Alexander Cycle, only to cite one group of parallels, we find the same desolate wastes and extraordinary mountains, as well as the flight up into the skies which Chaucer knew and mentions. The alliterative *Wars*, which tells of Alexander's flight with the griffons, also describes a "wilsom waste and wild and wondirly cold," and a valley "where flakes of snow fall from heaven" and "sparks of fire fall like rain," recalling distinctly the desert scene in the *Inferno*, which Chaucer himself remembered. With such descriptions at hand one may ask why Chaucer failed to write an actual romance. Perhaps he was more concerned with his search for tidings. Perhaps, as in the case of the Knight, his humor was far too mischievous when he told this story.

The fact remains that there seem to have been odd moments when he, too, held Lancelot de Lake in full great reverence, or had, at least, a glimpse of things romantic of which the spell still lingers here and there in his poetry. Any creature of the land-beyond-the-mist would testify to the "authentic note" sounded in such a description as that of the scene

> . . . under a forest syde,
> Wher as he saugh upon a daunce go
> Of ladyes foure and twenty, and yet mo;
> Toward the whiche daunce he drow ful yerne,
> In hope that som wysdom sholde he lerne.

But certeinly, er he cam fully there,
Vanysshed was this daunce, he nyste where.

                                D. 990–996.

This charming episode he borrowed (I suppose from
Walter Map) like many another; but that does not affect
the point. One reason that definitions of romance have been
so difficult to agree upon is that a prime essential of the romantic is its elusiveness. Is it pedantic to hint that this is
what marks the hovering quality in such passages in Chaucer's verse? The words themselves have magic. As Logan
Pearsall Smith observed regarding some poetry that moved
him, "Such lines open for me portals into realms of beauty
and fear and strangeness. . . ." At any rate it is no disparage-
ment to claim that Chaucer, like many another, looked
through magic casements in his day, and that his realism was
none the worse for it.

Chapter IX

THE SATIRIST

THE SATIRIST is an incalculable person. His moral purpose may be best served in his opinion by throwing wide of the mark. On the other hand, though he hits the moral bull's eye again and again, he may have little real interest in producing any effect other than laughter or aesthetic enjoyment. "The true end of satire is the amendment of vices by correction," said Dryden, and doubtless that was his own high principle. But at least one critic has maintained that so great a satirist as Molière cared for moral issues only as strands in the fine tissue of his irony. If, as Dryden further observes, Persius insulted his victims rather than exposed vice or folly, it was probably because the Latin poet cared more for the poisonous joy of attack than for reform. The truth is that the satirist may have several purposes; he may kill two birds with one stone and yet have another bird in the hand at the same time. It all depends on what his attitude toward his public may chance to be. He may be fundamentally irresponsible and furnish nothing more than delight in the accuracy of his shots, or he may be deeply in earnest and aim most of all to edify; but the power and richness of his satiric gifts will not determine the intention that informs his art.

These gifts and that intention will be partly a matter of temperament. Satirists are born, not made. Despite all manner of silliness in the juvenilia of Jane Austen one can tell that their author is destined to write with a sharp pen whatever her motive. There is an intuitive touch in *Frederic and Elfrida* where the "aged gentleman with a sallow face & old pink Coat" fell at Charlotte's feet and declared his attachment to her: "Not being able to resolve to make any one miserable, she consented to become his wife. . . ." The child who could write thus saw life in a peculiar way that encourages a smile. This is the young person who later in life could also write: "This morning we have been to see Miss Chamberlayne look hot on horseback." In fact I believe the mark of the genuine, dyed-in-the-wool satirist is this way of sizing things up and then of expressing the idea with extraordinary succinctness and sharpness. That is why she or he so often finds the heroic couplet a neat and fitting medium for what there is to say:

> But in love's voyage nothing can offend;
> Women are never seasick with a friend.
> > Dryden's rendering of Juvenal.

> He sought the storms; but, for a calm unfit,
> Would steer too nigh the sands, to boast his wit.
> > *Absalom and Achitophel.*

We know of old the clink of this coin. But the same edge is possible in prose: "Being a light-complexioned woman, she wore light clothes, as most blondes will, and appeared, in preference, in draggled sea-green, or slatternly sky-blue" (*Vanity Fair*). Meredith could never get over his fascination for achieving this effect; he lets Mrs. Mounstuart say of Letitia Dale: "Here she comes with a romantic tale on her eyelashes. . . ." Henry James does it perfectly for Miss Birds-eye: ". . . in her faded face there was a kind of reflexion of ugly lecture-lamps. . . ." These are what people call swift strokes, and they indicate the congenital writer of satire.

Everyone knows how naturally and easily Chaucer does this kind of thing. The quotations are famous. Of the Lawyer he tells us:

> Nowher so bisy a man as he ther nas,
> And yet he semed bisier than he was.
>   A. 321–322.

Of the Doctor:

> He kepte that he wan in pestilence.
> For gold in phisik is a cordial,
> Therefore he lovede gold in special.
>   A. 442–444.

Of the Miller:

> His mouth as greet was as a greet forneys.
> He was a janglere and a goliardeys,
> And that was moost of synne and harlotries.
>   A. 559–561.

His patterns, as these lines will show, do not stop as a rule with the couplet. Perhaps because he is not chiefly interested in killing, he makes a point but does not end with the thrust of the rhyme. As the thought often runs over into the next line or so, the derogatory element is often supplemented by a favorable observation. So of the Friar we have the final reference to his eyes twinkling like stars on a frosty night; and the Lawyer knows his law, and the Miller can blow a good note on the bagpipe. Chaucer does not appear to be irked by the faults he reveals in his characters. Unlike Juvenal and Persius, Dryden and Pope and Swift, he does not give evidence of being unhappy about them or of holding a lash in readiness. I cannot find that, however much he remains conscious of vice as vice, he has expectation of making people over by his ridicule. Perhaps this is the subtlest method of teaching, but it is not the procedure of most satirists. Indeed one is inclined to think that these ironic touches appear in his portraits simply because he saw life in this way.

If this is how he saw life, as he sat in the Custom House, walked to and fro, paid visits to royalty and nobility, left London on his travels to visit other great cities of men, and in his solitude of spirit, perhaps, leaned on his elbows looking out at the world, still it cannot be said that on his features dwelt the "slim feasting smile" of which Meredith has told us. Take for example some lines in the description of the lady Prioress:

> She leet no morsel from hir lippes falle,
> Ne wette hir fyngres in hir sauce depe;
> Wel koude she carie a morsel and wel kepe
> That no drope ne fille upon hire brest.

And so on (A. 128 ff.) In other words she does all that according to the books of etiquette and the *Roman de la Rose* she ought to do. We can see her exquisite hand making a lovely curve in the air as it conveys that morsel to her mouth "ful smal, and therto softe and reed." The comic spirit nibbles a little here no doubt. But if I understand Meredith's expression, the feasting smile suggests the lean and merciless. Moreover, if this passage just quoted has a delicacy appropriate to the lady it describes, even in the cases of the coarser figures, like the Friar and the Summoner and the Miller (the Pardoner always excepted), the satire is not truly mordant. The innuendoes in the portrait of the Friar, the Summoner's generosity regarding concubines, the Miller's foul talk, over such things the poet hardly licks his lips. He presents them as part of life, as Rabelais might, like dirt and dung and belching sewers. This is true also of the more violent satire in some of the stories like the *Reeve's Tale* and the *Summoner's Tale*. At least most of this is more in the manner of Horace than of Juvenal or Persius, in that of Fielding rather than that of Swift or Thackeray.

Whether a satirist punishes or exposes or merely reveals may be simply a matter of physical response, like some product of the humors — as one might expect in the case of a predominance of phlegm or bile. Fielding is not always merciful; one can see that much in his attack on the hypocrisy of Mr. Blifil's suit for the hand of Sophia: "In doing this he availed himself of the piety of Thwackum, who held, that if the end proposed was religious (as surely matrimony is), it mattered not how wicked were the means." But the universe is not poisoned by his hatred as it sometimes appears to be in Thackeray's cosmic scorn: "The brandy-bottle inside clinked up against the plate which held the cold sausage. Both were moved, no doubt, by the exhibition of so much grief" (*Vanity Fair*). In contrast Fielding's mood is usually that of one who is pretty well satisfied with life, as we may see in his "short hint of what [he] can do in the sublime," and the description of Sophia Western: "Do thou, sweet Zephyrus, rising from thy fragrant bed, mount the western sky, and lead on those delicious gales, the charms

of which call forth the lovely Flora from her chamber, per-
fumed with pearly dews, when on the 1st of June, her birth-
day, the blooming maid, in loose attire, gently trips it over
the verdant mead, where every flower rises to do her homage, till the whole field becomes enamelled, and colours con-
tend with sweets which shall ravish her most." And then of
Miss Sophia: ". . . Her eyebrows were full, even, and arched
beyond the power of art to imitate. . . . Her complexion
had rather more of the lily than of the rose. . . ." The tone
of all this is precisely that of the description of Emelye's first
appearance:

> Till it fil ones, in a morwe of May,
> That Emelye, that fairer was to sene
> Than is the lylie upon his stalke grene,
> And fressher than the May with floures newe —
> For with the rose colour stroof hire hewe,
> I noot which was the fyner of hem two —

And so on, and so on (A. 1034 ff.). The cheerful ease in both
cases makes me think of the rather irresponsible facility and
good temper of Ariosto, and shows the reason, I think, why
for a long time people classified Chaucer as belonging to the
Renaissance. It is a manner, however, shared more or less by
Giraldus Cambrensis, Walter Map, certain authors of the
Carmina Burana, the writer of the *Pèlerinage de Charlemagne*, and many others of the Middle Ages.

Chaucer digests life with a relish. The background of
nature in his stories is filled, as a rule, with sunshine. The
gods get in a flutter now and then, as in the *Knight's Tale* and
the *Merchant's Tale*, when their wires are crossed; but no
slightest suggestion is forthcoming that they glare about with

malevolence, not even when in the one case Dame Venus
and in the other Proserpine put it completely over on the
males who oppose them. I don't know exactly why Chaucer
sees the universe as so very happy when, as a matter of fact,
his stories are filled with adulteries, trickery and dirty cheating, bad smells of all kinds, but it must have been because of
his faith. I am reminded of what Firkins wrote about Jane
Austen: "I think she portrayed truth, when she did portray
truth, because she liked it — *really* liked it — without theory
and without conscience. . . . It is good to be natural in one's
love of nature." So Chaucer accepted the whole picture as
he found it, and thought it good.

But all this sounds like the very opposite of the attitude
of your robust, full-bellied satirist, does it not? For when I
say that Chaucer accepted the picture, I really mean that he
seems to be fairly complacent as if the whole drama is great
fun, and as if it doesn't much matter whether there is anything wrong about it. This spirit prevails in the *House of
Fame* in the representation of the various types that come to
Fame asking for her gifts. It appears again in the wrangling
of the birds in the *Parliament*. It forms the chief pattern in
the tragedy of Troilus, when all is said and done; the youth
suffered, but then all shall pass at length and there is many a
smile along the way. So too with the *Legend*, where certainly there is no hint of a corrective intention (except —
and this is out of the picture — the advice to the God of Love
about tyrants). And with the *Canterbury Tales* it can hardly
be thought that Chaucer's portraits of the Monk and the
Nun would have their due effect on contemporary monastic
discipline, or that millers and summoners would be casti-

gated by echoes of what he said about their trade. In fact he hardly seems to have tried to reach them personally. A young squire at Court hearing the account of his type might have been embarrassed to recognize it but could scarcely have put by the humor of his youth. The most we can say is that there may be a general effect of this kind of satire which slowly and intangibly makes its deep impression because it shows that the poet has an uncompromising sense of moral values. Chaucer did not write his *Troilus* to warn young ladies not to be Cressidas; yet, for all the poet's avowed attempt to let her off, Criseyde's guilt shows its stain and her memory is not wholly pleasant in the reader's mind.

But this is reckoning only with details. How about the broader outlines of Chaucer's work as revealed by his method of handling his sources? Let us take, for one example, the *Franklin's Tale*, where, I have come to feel pretty sure, he is making over the story as Boccaccio gave it to the world in the *Filocolo*. The task imposed on the ardent suitor in Boccaccio's version is to produce a garden blooming in January. I have often thought with astonishment that Chaucer missed some fine strokes of irony in not keeping this garden when he came to the point of adapting the tale for the purposes of the Franklin. The Merchant had already told of one fine garden, one that offered associations and fragrances that were certain to last through several other stories on the pilgrimage. Now if the ardent squire who wooed Dorigen had been told by her to achieve the magic of creating one of these flowery meads in the middle of winter's chill what delicious suggestions would have been added thereby, what overtones beyond the hearing of Dorigen herself and indeed that of

the young squire! But Chaucer, I suppose, thought the task
of covering the rocks more truly symbolized Dorigen's love
for her husband, and threw the emphasis in that way on this
love rather than on the squire's passion. In other words
this lady's lovely devotion meant more to him than the
flashes and side glances of humor in the suitor's desire and
its parallel to that of Damian in the *Merchant's Tale*. This
point is the more valid in that the poet seems to have written
the two stories at about the same time and to have tied up all
the items in the Marriage Cycle with echoes and cross-
references.

On the other hand we can see Chaucer altering his plot
to achieve a more satiric effect in another instance. In the
Wife of Bath's Tale his source probably did not include the
initial episode of the rape for which the knight is punished
by the search. In Gower's form of the story and in others we
do not find this crime. As we now have it from the Wife of
Bath herself it serves many purposes. It reflects first of all on
the teller of the story, and receives a reflection from her.
What did the Wife think of rape in the catalogue of crimes?
— I am afraid, if she were honest, she would have admitted
that it was, like stories of atrocity in wartime and the atroc-
ities themselves (some of them), "ful blisful." And then the
fact that Guinivere is sufficiently touched by the knight's sad
case, and sufficiently sympathetic, to furnish him with a way
of escape, this too is not without its mild flavor. And finally
the task itself, the search for the answer to the question what
it is that women most desire, is the perfect fulfilment of the
ironic opportunities of the episode: for, in the first place, one
is tempted to guess that what women most desire is what the

original victim of the rape so forcibly got; and secondly, the right answer, mastery over man, is for the Wife of Bath and also in general the complete corrective to the original misdemeanor. Thus the poet here manipulated his plot in order to introduce certain extra qualities of satire which were not in his source. But his purpose was not primarily to teach. The irony here does not castigate sexual license or foolish young men; in its power of enrichment for the story, while it adds enormously to the scene where the poor knight is turning and twisting in bed with the old crone to avoid her (he who once had made war on chastity), it extends the radiance of the humor of the Wife of Bath and contributes to her portrait. Most of all, I personally believe, this irony affords its own marvellous entertainment to the reader.

Did Chaucer ever alter his source to bring in an element of satire for the purpose of teaching or reform? I cannot think of an instance. Perhaps that is what he did in making over material for the *Friar's Tale* of the corrupt summoner. I have a confident suspicion that Chaucer is himself responsible for the wonderful thrust where the Friar says of his leading character:

> He dorste nat, for verray filthe and shame
> Seye that he was a somonour, for the name.
>   D. 1393–1394.

Score ten for the Friar! But the poet here gives his readers pleasure rather than reaches the summoners of his day with moral effect. He would abolish the type, I have no doubt, just as he would stir moral indignation against the whole class of pardoners; but Chaucer did not go to Rome to or-

ganize a movement for appeal to the Pope. For him, in all
this, it might almost be said that the moral values furnish
simply another color in his design. But that is not so. If he
is anywhere open to the age-old charge of naïveté it is in the
way in which he includes the edifying and uplifting stories
as part of his collection on the way to Canterbury; they heap
up the *satura lanx*. It is almost as if he had thought he must
have stories moral as well as stories ribald. But the writer
who once had translated all of *Melibee* and compiled the substance of the *Parson's Tale* sees morality as something more
than an aesthetic value in art. He may even be accused of
having moral purposes in his writing. My point here, however, is that in his satire and in his humor his spontaneity
does not primarily include a desire to rectify or change.
What he sees in life he affirms.

The fact is that he does not bring forth satiric elements in
his work at all. They are there because they represent part of
his nature, an important part of his outlook on the world.
So when he consciously intends to be instructive or edifying,
as in the *Tale of Melibee* or the *Clerk's Tale*, he very often sur-
rounds the moral with a setting of humor, which may even
go so far as very nearly to discount the moral purpose. So
it is in the first example he pokes fun at this "tretys lyte,"
and in the second gives us the whole background of the controversy with the Wife of Bath. In such a framework too we
find the sermon on democracy in the bedroom scene of the
Wife of Bath's Tale. On the other hand there is a quite ingenu-
ous simplicity in the presentation of the tales of the Man of
Law, the Prioress, the Physician, the Second Nun, and the
Parson. With these stories it is all pretty solemn, as far as the

manner of the speaker is concerned. In consequence the poet is here not half so truly the mirror of "fructuous entendement" that he is elsewhere (even if the story of the Prioress is a masterpiece) because here his full nature is not giving itself freely. His best manner is when he is setting forth something morally sound with humorous detachment, as in the scene where Dorigen complains and gives her own particular legend of good women, the catalogue of chaste wives. Did the poet mean that catalogue to be merely instructive and the scene to be nothing more than pathetic? The Franklin did, I have no doubt. But Chaucer knew that the Wife of Bath was one of the auditors, and he remembered her views of chastity. And Dorigen's unceasing flow is like the Canon's Yeoman's exhibitionism of his stock in trade; she simply cannot stop listing chaste wives, even when she has reached her conclusion (F. 1422–1423): "Thus pleyned Dorigen a day or tweye" (F. 1457).

I suspect that it is somewhat in the same way that the poet produces that finest flowering of narrative art — dramatic irony. In other words it appears in his work because it represents the way in which he saw life in general, and it was therefore inevitable. It is spontaneous; it seems to be neither a conscious artifice nor touched with any definite purpose didactic or revealing. It is, moreover, extraordinarily rich in implication. Dramatic irony may be successful enough with only one extra layer of meaning: we see it at work when, for instance, Criseyde bids Troilus to be forever true to her, and we know at that very moment that she will ultimately betray him. But Chaucer has the skill to achieve more than just the one flashing ray at one time. Like medieval allegory

which builds up not only a literal meaning but the moral
and spiritual and even other interpretations as well, his irony
is sometimes many-faceted and sends forth varied colors in
a single situation.

It comes quite naturally and simply again and again into
his work. In the *Franklin's Tale*, which I have just been
discussing, there are some fine examples. The story opens
with a reference to "maistrye" and the statement that
Arviragus and Dorigen will have none of it: with them love
is to be free. But the time comes when Aurelius accomplishes
the magic task of removing the rocks and thanks Phebus and
Venus for his triumph: he thinks he has won his victim.
Moreover, it is to be noted that the rocks are actually removed *after* the return of Arviragus from his long journey
and when the need has itself vanished. Dorigen, however,
feels she is caught, and in her long soliloquy says that she
prefers death to dishonor, or rather — more accurately:

> "I wol be trewe unto Arveragus,
> Or rather sleen myself in som manere . . ."
>
> F. 1424–1425.

Yet, once we have read the story, we know at this time that
she will soon be walking down the road to the garden where
she is supposed to meet Aurelius, and this at her husband's
bidding. Could *maistrye* go further? How free is love when it
is thus constrained to infidelity — or is it infidelity? She prefers death to dishonor and will be true to Arviragus, yes, but
what does "true" mean in such a context? And for that matter what does love mean? Is there anything more amusing
in the world than Dorigen on her way to the miserable garden saying to her potential lover that she is going —

"Unto the gardyn, as myn housbonde bad,
My trouthe for to holde, allas! allas!"

F. 1512–1513.

As I have suggested, the garden itself catches up some of the
associations prepared for it in the *Merchant's Tale*. And so in
many ways the passage flashes a variety of ironic meanings
which convey one thing to Dorigen, another to Aurelius
(who must have had mixed emotions), and another, including all of these, to us. Among the last of these is what we gain
from knowing even at this point that Aurelius is going to let
her off, and so the irony, like that in certain parts of the
Clerk's Tale, is not of the sinister sort but — as we might
expect from the Franklin — positive, hopeful, implying
better things than the characters expect.

Such is not the case with that in the *Merchant's Tale*. There
is a story of successive strokes of sarcasm and bitter irony all
concentrated in episode and discussion. It should be considered not only for the light it throws on the Wife of
Bath's Prologue but as a companion piece to the *Franklin's
Tale*, which is almost its counterpart. Dorigen's *planctus* finds
its parallel in the Merchant's list of good women. The squire
and the garden are in both stories; matrimony is exalted in
one and debased in the other. The irony which the Merchant
offers, however, is cruel. Take, for example, the scene in
which January sends May to call on the sick Damian: this
young squire is sick with nothing more than love; January
will expect her back when she comes to bed. "Dooth hym
disport — he is a gentil man," says the poor old fool (E.
1924). To himself the command doubtless seems generous;
to May it is at this time irksome; to us it has a different light
from what follows. There are many points of the keenest

irony in the Merchant's telling of this story, but one more may suffice. Take the exultant song of January almost ready to start on the way to his garden on the fateful day. He chooses to echo, nay to quote, as we have observed, the Song of Songs, which in the Church had the most sacred of associations as prognosticating the union of Christ with His holy Bride. It is many-faceted, this passage: it calls up the absurd little garden that January has had constructed to guard his spouse from others and to keep her for himself, which nevertheless serves to bring May and the squire together; it sets forth January's passion in the most exalted figures, and the more they are exalted and the more they recall January's passion so the greater is their bathos; their celestial fragrance, like that of certain passages in the Gospel according to St John, becomes in this context something more pungent and less heavenly, partly because we know that May will not praise this chanting worth a bean; and the lyric pitch of January's excitement is all the more ridiculous as well as foul because we know what lies ahead.

It is in the freshness of the morning that old January sings:

"Rys up, my wyf, my love, my lady free!
The turtles voys is herd, my dowve sweete;
The wynter is goon with alle his reynes weete.
Com forth now, with thyne eyen columbyn!
How fairer been thy brestes than is wyn!
The gardyn is enclosed al aboute;
Com forth, my white spouse! out of doute
Thou hast me wounded in myn herte, O wyf!
No spot of thee ne knew I al my lyf.
Com forth, and lat us taken oure disport;
I chees thee for my wyf and my confort."
E. 2138–2148.

And a moment later Damian's hand is on the "cliket" that opens the garden "wyket" (and with the rhyme we hear him enter). In all literature is there any irony, I wonder, more savage than this. January is not simply a pitiable old lecher; he has become, through his sarcasm, his lyric power, his rational self-justification, the embodiment of desire in old age, and so an important type. He is less poetic, of course, than Merlin surrounded by the magic circle of Vivian's enchantment; but he is none the less real in the way he gathers up all the unsavory traits of licentious age in the odor of his own personality. Thus with the background of the gods working out his destiny, with Proserpine getting neatly around Pluto, and the promise that henceforth all women shall have their answers pat, there is something truly epic in quality in the old man's ecstasy. It is irony set to music.

Of all the aspects of Chaucer's greatness there are few more important than this gift of presenting strokes of rich ironic value. As we can see in the *Merchant's Tale* he does it with the most amazing ease. Not alone one charge of significance is what carries the scene, but several at one time. Moreover in the episode we have just touched upon this extraordinary power is increased by the fact that the scene is described by the Merchant; and, as the Merchant shows this mordant exposure of January, every line of it recoils ironically upon himself. It is his sexual frustration that lends bitterness to the story; it is he as well as January who is fooled in the singing of this song: he remembers the dovelike eyes and the fair breasts, and curses their beauty herewith, and even so he too is on his way to the enclosed garden with Solomon's love song on his lips. Such, at least in our imaginations as we listen to his story, is the figure he cuts. "My beloved is gone down into his garden, to the beds of spices, to feed in the gardens, and to gather lilies."

There is a variety in Chaucer's ironies that corresponds to his range of appeal in general. The examples in the *Merchant's Tale* show a corrosive, destructive, even a hopeless quality, not unmixed with hatred, and the very opposite of the optimistic instances in the story told by the Franklin. I have already compared these latter with the similar examples in the story of Griselda, where, in the same way, the overtone of meaning carries the realization that matters are much better than Griselda can know. Something like pathos is here; but here are still other overtones created by the setting in the give and take of the Marriage Cycle, and so Griselda's unfaltering obedience has certain elements of reflected humor in it and the irony another layer of meaning. Pathos almost by itself, on the other hand, is found in the irony of the scene in the *Man of Law's Tale*, where King Alla in ignorance asks with approval about his own child: here too things are better than he can suppose. Of the same type is that where the senator praises Constance to Alla unaware of the fact she is the King's wife. Irony of the pessimistic sort, however, made up of pathos appears in the *Prioress's Tale* where the little scholar fears he may suffer punishment for learning the *Alma Redemptoris* — he may even get a beating! Thus there are many flavors in the poet's irony, as there are differences in its depth and in its richness. One can find it in nearly all his works, except perhaps where saintly figures are described whose will is so close to union with the divine intent that irony is out of place.

The most charming examples, I think, with almost a complete range of quality, are found in *Troilus and Criseyde*. Here the poet has more than one string to his bow; sometimes indeed the overtones suggest the fine playing of a string-quartet or even greater orchestral accomplishment. It is possible, of course, to read the poem without catching any of this music, as some people seem to have read the *Nun's Priest's Tale* without detecting its humor. The *Troilus* affords at least a good story on the lowest level of understanding. There will always be dispute about what its author meant, and how much he meant, as there must be in the case of any literary work of art. But without attempting to be dogmatic in the matter, we may lay it down as a wise principle that the interpretation which yields the richest results is on the face of things likely to be the truest where a major work of art is concerned. The burden of proof is less with him who reads the deepest significance into a poem than with him who sets down limits. The task of the critic, I would maintain, is judiciously to be *feliciter audax*. But I feel that it takes less courage than might be supposed to expound the fullest values of the *Troilus*, the only question really being whether the critic is competent to discover all its excellences at their full value. I believe that it takes a critic of the same genius as the poet to reach all the imaginative limits of the poem. And if this observation seem unduly bold, I may qualify it by adding that a perfect understanding of Chaucer's intent in this case awaits realization, and will await it for some years to come, while much printed matter flows under the bridge. That is a delightful phase of the poem's objectivity.

Meanwhile there is no harm in offering our own present

ideas on the subject. Much is fairly certain at the outset. Thus when Criseyde demands assurance of Troilus's fidelity, no reader can miss the irony:

> "And that ye me wolde han as faste in mynde
> As I have yow, that wolde I yow biseche;
> And if I wiste sothly that to fynde,
> God myghte nought a poynt my joies eche."
>
> iii, 1506–1509.

In the beauty of the moment and Cressid's obvious sincerity, there is pathos in this appeal. Knowing what will spring from her weakness, however, we find something more grim in her complaint when she faces the problem of separation from her lover:

> She seyde, "How shal he don, and ich also?
> How sholde I lyve, if that I from hym twynne?"
>
> iv, 757–758.

Well, we know how she will live, and so does everybody; and the knowledge colors our reading of her whole lament:

> "To what fyn sholde I lyve and sorwen thus?
> How sholde a fissh withouten water dure?
> What is Criseyde worth, from Troilus?"
>
> iv, 764–766.

Another quality appears in the irony of her speech when she has left Troy and is gazing back upon its towers and halls. Not long before this we have seen Troilus visiting her empty house and looking from the walls of the city toward the Greek camp: "Lo, yonder is myn owene lady free," he said. And now Cressid, on the other side (perhaps some days later), looks back:

"O Troilus, what dostow now?" she seyde.
"Lord! wheyther thow yet thenke upon Criseyde?"

v, 734-735.

There is obvious humor in the mixture. But these are all simple examples, varied as they are. Something subtler perhaps is found in Troilus's line, when he stands recalling his lady's departure: "And yond I saugh hire to hire fader ride" (v, 612); we are likely to remember that she rode off with Diomede, who began at once to make love to her. Something of the sort there is also in Diomede's pledge of fidelity to Criseyde in that very scene:

"Yeve me youre hond; I am, and shal ben ay,
God helpe me so, while that my lyf may dure,
Youre owene aboven every creature."

v, 152-154.

The changes rung on the theme of fidelity in this poem are extraordinary, and it furnishes the essential unity of the story by touching every episode.

The promise Diomede makes to Cressid is anticipated in the similar vow that Troilus made on his own first meeting with her:

... "God woot, for I have,
As ferforthly as I have had konnynge,
Ben youres al, God so my soule save,
And shal, til that I, woful wight, be grave!"

iii, 100-103.

So as one turns the pages one may discover many points of irony that have to do with the same idea. Here we may note

the words with which Pandarus originally congratulated the
hero on his love:

> "Love hath byset the wel; be of good cheere!"
>
> i, 879.

> "So oughtest thou, for nought but good it is
> To loven wel, and in a worthy place;
> The oughte nat to clepe it hap, but grace."
>
> i, 894–896.

> "And thynk wel, she of whom rist al thi wo
> Hereafter may thy comfort be also."
>
> i, 944–945.

So all of Pandarus's efforts to bring his friend to bliss have
something of the same quality, especially in his own excitement. Sharper still is the feeling in Cressid's own review of
the situation, in which she tries to decide whether she will
give herself up to this affair or not:

> ". . . ek men ben so untrewe,
> That, right anon as cessed is hire lest,
> So cesseth love, and forth to love a newe."
>
> ii, 786–788.

> "How ofte tyme hath it yknowen be,
> The tresoun that to wommen hath ben do!"
>
> ii, 792–793.

Still richer irony appears in certain details, as, for example, in
the request of Deiphebus that Troilus come to the help of the
heroine:

> Deiphebus had hym preied over nyght
> To ben a frend and helpyng to Criseyde.
>
> ii, 1549–1550.

Here Chaucer points it by adding, "God woot that he it graunted anonright. . . ." But there is another layer of meaning here that may escape notice, unless we observe that by thus lending his help to his lady Troilus brings on his own doom; she becomes a treacherous friend to him. Here is what I have called the optimistic type of irony, but now it has a bitter relish. So too has Helen's greeting to him: "Now, faire brother, beth al hool, I preye!" (ii, 1670.)

Lines such as these have a complex of associations and meanings. But even at the risk of apparent surrender to those who will charge us with reading too much into such a scene, I hesitate to lay bare all the nerves that carry its vitality. The more one reads the poem the more one has the pleasure of finding in it new parallels, new reflections, new rays of the ironic interplay between one character and another, one scene and another. I shall limit myself here to pointing out an especially delicious form of optimistic irony of the sort peculiar to the *Troilus*. Pandarus has pleaded for his friend with the reluctant Criseyde, but she warns him:

> "And here I make a protestacioun,
> That in this proces if ye depper go,
> That certeynly, for no salvacioun
> Of yow, though that ye sterven bothe two,
> Though al the world on o day be my fo,
> Ne shal I nevere of hym han other routhe." —
> "I graunte wel," quod Pandare, "by my trowthe."
>
> ii, 484–490.

What is it she offers? "Myn honour sauf," she will "plese hym fro day to day." This is what she has just said. But of course we know that Pandarus and Troilus will want more,

and she will grant it. And what is more, she must be aware
that she will grant it — or at least a part of her is aware.
For it is not long before she asks, "Kan he wel speke of love?"
(ii, 503.) The fact is, all through this scene she tries ostensibly
to deceive Pandarus, and he tries ostensibly to deceive her.
But she partly knows that he understands her real intent,
and she is partly aware that he is conscious of her knowing
this. Here two worldly wise people save their faces by what
they say, and convey their real thoughts by overtones. Not
for an instant is Pandarus ever plunged into real discourage-
ment by Cressid's rebukes and warnings. That is why in a
later scene he dares to thrust the letter into her bosom and
knows she will read it and answer it. That is also why, when
later Pandarus invites the lady to his house on the rainy
night, she is perfectly sure that Troilus is there, but does not
tell herself so. The music that we get from these magnificent
characters has more than two voices.

It is well that *Troilus and Criseyde* has often been studied as
drama; for it has so much of that prime essential of dramatic art, irony based on action and interaction. In contrast
with familiar examples, such as that of Oedipus in search of
the criminal who has brought the curse upon Thebes, it
shows something far less grim. But it has amazing variety in
form and quality. And we are so used to such implications
in Criseyde's speech that the effect carries over into one expression of hers where we cannot really know its full value
because we do not know the future: that is when she says,
"To Diomede algate I wol be trewe" (v, 1071). This desperate cry has an ironic power in spite of her purpose. Thus
it is no exaggeration to say that without a perception of this

element in the poem one is bound to miss the best it has to offer. The contrast between the intention of the character and the full meaning of the scene as we the audience know it gives us that sense of fundamental incongruity on which full emotional response must in part be based. It is thus that we understand the references to love and the lyrics and the Epilogue according to the theme that runs through the poem and unites its parts. But its irony is never heavy, because, as with the *Knight's Tale*, it is a story of youth; nor is it as bitter as that in the *Merchant's Tale*, because there the narrator hated his heroine. It is not calculated to drive home a lesson; it is too sympathetic for that. It is rather the expression of a detached and mature and realistic mind, equable enough to observe that all shall pass and that odd things occur along the way. *Othello* has fiercer moments, no doubt, and *Samson Agonistes* strikes deeper notes. But Chaucer's manipulation of dramatic irony, of humor, of the satiric touch, shows a range and a richness as great as anything his incomparable imagination offers. It reveals not only his scope and versatility but also his power. The poet's humor itself, or whatever it is that we have considered in that rather loose category, is a sign of the health and fullness of his wisdom.

Chapter X

THE DEVELOPMENT OF
CHAUCER'S GENIUS

ANY CRITICAL or biographical study which attempts to indicate something of the nature of a poet's personal development is arbitrary to a certain degree and likely to be fantastic. Only the psychologist, with the assistance of the philosopher, the doctor, and the specialist in dietetics perhaps, and with a vast array of detailed records, could really hope to plot out the general lines which the career of any genius really has followed. Indeed I have thought of calling this chapter "Geoffrey Chaucer and how he grew," to suggest on the side the palpable absurdity of trying to undertake a study of anything of the sort. But inevitably and laudably critics have expended some effort on such a task with certain results which occasionally seem profitable, and with others which I believe to be entirely mistaken. My present purpose is to comment on these views, in somewhat the manner perhaps of some semi-popular address entitled "Chaucer the man," as a possible method of getting a general summary of the ideas I have here set forth. Perhaps in the negative tone of these concluding remarks it will appear that I have moved from dreamlike considerations and a trace of the poetic in the early chapters to a realistic approach and finally in the present case to a cynical attitude. If so, there will be an aesthetic appropriateness in the fact;

for such is the nature of Chaucer's development according to some critics.

To show how opinion varies on these matters I may quote Mr. A. W. Pollard's remarks: "[Chaucer's] early poems are very beautiful, but they are sentimental and a little weak, with hardly a trace of humour and no great power of characterisation. In his later poems sentiment is replaced by a not unkindly cynicism; his sense of the beauty of religion has perhaps not diminished, but he himself is less religious and grosser; his subtle humour has become infinite, and with a few masterly strokes he portrays a character to the life." Now to designate the early poems as "sentimental and a little weak, with hardly a trace of humour" — if we mean to refer to the *Parliament of Fowls* and the *House of Fame*, or even the *Book of the Duchess* — is, I believe, as completely to miss the mark as it is possible for critical aberration to do. The *Book of the Duchess* accomplishes its task by the very miracle of its being loaded with sentiment and yet not sentimental but humorous. As allegories of the Court of Love go, all three of these poems are not only anything but weak (by which I suppose that Mr. Pollard really means somewhat insipid); they are rich with meaning, at times even packed with delicious effect. I think, for example, of the account of the gates in the *Parliament* and also of the squabble of the birds, and also of the flight in the *House of Fame*. But these things hardly need to be said; or if they do, there is no use in saying them. I find myself unable to comment on the idea that with age Chaucer became less religious and grosser; for it is quite possible that he did. I can imagine his faithful attendance at the confessional box year after year (one critic concedes that the poet may have kept faithful to his religious duties once a year), with the consequent realization on his part of no advance and even of an increase in physical girth rather than of spiritual agility. I do maintain, however, that there is no slightest trace of evidence on this point one way or another. In the Wife of Bath's Prologue and in the *Merchant's Tale* not a single line, not a single detail, has anything to reveal on this score. Even January's quoting the *Song of Solomon* does not tell us that the poet was less interested than of old in attaining some day to the beatific vision.

Nor does it show any taint of cynicism. With reference to such a charge I prefer ten Brink's analysis of Chaucer's development: ". . . formerly he moved in a world of dreams or in unattainable idealism; but now [in his later years] he prefers to stand upon the ground of reality, and, with the necessary variations, to treat of things recent and local. The preponderance of the comic element in the later effusions of his Muse depends largely on this change to realism, as does also the prevalence of the heroic couplet for the form of his verse. . . ." Let me parenthetically protest, first of all, against that phrase "the effusions of his Muse" (for which, I suppose, ten Brink was not responsible), which to my own imagination calls up something forbidding. I do not find in Chaucer's early work signs of an "unattainable idealism." But the main idea is sound — the poet's works do show a greater emphasis on what is called the realistic as the years move on. Because of literary fashion he began with the allegorical and the abstract and the somewhat typical; more and more he adopted stories and characters that carried a more immediate reference to his own experience. But that is true only in general. In the allegories there is much that is realistic and the spirit of comedy is never wholly absent, even if in the *Legend* her smile is wan, and in the first part of the *Book of the Duchess* she is often silent. In the early works we have the same Geoffrey Chaucer that appears to us later: sane, realistic, steady, possessed of that detachment which shows itself in humor. His growth is in the direction of more realism and more humor. The realism for him (because that is how he was built) releases the humor. But in all this there is nothing that hints of cynicism.

The poet began by being naïf, we are told, and ended by being cynical. I can hardly imagine two adjectives more absurdly applied. I doubt whether Geoffrey Chaucer was ever naïf, and I will hold to that observation even while I read and reread his *Tale of Melibee* and the *Parson's Tale* and his stories of Constance and Virginia and Griselda and Cecilia. There may be a self-deceiving cultivation of emotion for its own sake in his telling of the sufferings of these four latter heroines, but I doubt it; I have already discussed something of this problem. Yet as he kept these narratives for inclusion in the *Canterbury Tales*, by the same token his own nature may contain such elements of simplicity and be at the same time greater and more inclusive than any of them. Whatever his early works may be, they are certainly not naïf. If anyone ever took the machinery of Courtly Love with literal faith and devout spirit, such an attitude might be so described; but there is no evidence that anyone ever did. In general, literature that employs this material may be inept or perhaps dull, but in its own occasionally tawdry way it is sophisticated. Its allegorical analysis forces a degree of self-consciousness. And Chaucer's use is that of an artist who is fully aware of what sort of apparatus he is borrowing; the special touch of humor he adds shows sophistication and a kind of maturity, a combination anything but naïf.

As Mr. Kittredge shows, the word as mistakenly here applied is especially ill chosen. "Whatever one may think of our American practice in the appointment of diplomatists," he remarks, "it is quite certain that, in the fourteenth century, men were not selected by the English king to negotiate secret affairs on the Continent because they were innocent and artless." The positions held by Chaucer reveal the confidence with which he was regarded by the men of his day, and they tell something as well of his urbanity of nature. Yet someone may object that successful business men are often naïf when it comes to a taste in literature. Even there, however, Chaucer shows his subtlety at once: in his compliment to the great Duke of Lancaster in the *Book of the Duchess*, and in the variety of his humor as he employs the artifices of the literature of Courtly Love. So if the poet early in his career shows this quality, his later indulgence (if such it is) in the simpler appeal of the *Tale of Melibee* and the story of Constance must be a temporary lapse, with a subsequent return to sophistication, say in the *Troilus* or some of the descriptions in the *General Prologue* of the *Canterbury Tales*, and then another lapse in *Trouthe* maybe, or at least the *Retractation*. If we date the *Man of Law's Tale* after the *General Prologue*, things become worse than ever. The poet is at one time sophisticated and again naïf, and we cannot exonerate him in terms of the subject matter he is using; for that varies and in any case the distinction is arbitrary. But

these suppositions are really pointless. A man is, I would insist, a generally unified creature; and in particular Chaucer
shows special signs of being highly integrated. It is unlikely
that he was naïf on Thursdays and sophisticated on the other
days of the week.

The chances are that the notion of his naïveté has arisen as
I have already suggested: it depends on our view of the
subject matter he employs. When he deals in moral treatises
or saints' legends the modern exclaims at his simplicity. But
we have clear evidence of what the poet thought of some
of this material in the setting he gave to the story of Melibeus
and to that of Griselda. In his day Petrarch was nothing if
not a highly sophisticated intellect, and to him the account
of patient Griselda was most affecting; yet the setting that
Chaucer finally gave it served to discount some of its moral
effect. If the placing of the *Tale of Melibee* after the burlesque
mood of the *Tale of Sir Thopas*, and the reference to it as
this "little treatise," do not suggest that it be taken with a
grain of salt, at least there is something of the air of a pinch
of snuff about it. The real point is that from time to time the
poet shows evidence of having taken his morals and religion
on authority, and we cannot forgive him such credulity until
he offers some signs of recanting. But he never really recants
anything that has to do with the faith. His attitude toward
the story of Melibeus and toward that of Griselda is natural
for a man who is at ease with his morals and his idealism. It
perplexes the modern to find him telling the hearty sensual
story of Troilus and Criseyde, and at the same time keeping
his moral judgments clear; but a Catholic can do that, or anyone whose religion is healthy. He does not compromise

morality by treating the stories of Melibeus and Griselda as he does; he only lets down their exaggerations. I fear we have no right at all to say that anyone in the fourteenth century who accepted Christian morality and saints' legends was naïf. Even in the *Retractation* Chaucer was not that. Perhaps he was frightened there, and he was probably sick. He may have had a momentary flash of insight into the values of purity and holiness, one that threw his sense of proportion out of joint. Far from being simple at this time he is more nearly subject to the charge of duplicity. But moderns will find it hard to understand how he undoubtedly escaped that.

What about the cynicism with which we are told he was much taken in later years? Such a retreat sounds a little childish, does it not? I have said elsewhere that quite possibly he went through a stage of disillusionment, but that is quite another matter. Illusions are not the alternative to cynicism; to suppose that, one would have to be truly naïf about life. I confess I do not know what illusions Chaucer cast off; perhaps some idea taken from the *dolce styl nuovo* that woman inevitably leads us upward and onward, perhaps some youthful notion that the ultimate satisfactions are those of Venus. He had emerged from the one by the time he wrote the *Troilus*, and from the other at least by the time he described the Wife of Bath. When the halfgods go, the gods arrive; and dispelling illusions releases the deeper and fuller vision. But cynicism implies, unless I much mistake, belief in very little of anything. It hints at sneering (an expression foreign to Chaucer, as Mr. Pollard's use of "not unkindly cynicism" shows he was aware) and it certainly means that the cynic is given to think poorly of his fellowmen. They are all, he would say, pretty much moved by self-interest. Now that view I do not find in Chaucer at any time. Some of his characters, some of his pilgrims, are moved by self-interest, but others (and some of these the products of his maturest work) are not. I do not believe it is fair to say this is wholly true of the Knight or the Franklin (in the *Prologue*), or even of the Monk or the Prioress or the Wife of Bath. But let us consider the Wife of Bath, whose self-revelation in her proem has been sometimes taken as the height of cynical expression.

There is really too much faith in it, too much virtue, for that. It shows, even on the Wife's part, too much belief in people and in life. There is more than sensuality in the Wife's love for her fifth husband. She likes to get the better of him, but also has something more than a masochistic delight when he has the upper hand. There is rich suggestion in their final agreement:

> But atte laste, with muchel care and wo,
> We fille acorded by us selven two.
> He yaf me al the bridel in myn hond . . .
> > D. 811–813.

It carries the idea of many a scene like that where he hit her for tearing three pages out of his book, and where she gave him a good blow in return. But she got her chance on that occasion because in penitence he knelt down and said:

> . . . "Deere suster Alisoun,
> As help me God! I shal thee nevere smyte."
> > D. 804–805.

He really loves her, and the whole scene is the more gorgeous because of the fact that these two brutal fighters love each other desperately. The pleasure of the story lies in no respect in an exhibition of folly or futility; no interpretation which reads this episode as the revelation of mere animalism, cruelty, or any other form of self-interest, is possible. So all through the Prologue the delight is in a humor based, not on the exposure of mere weakness, but on robustness or vitality or assumed candor, or perhaps always as well on the portrayal of the sound value of human nature in its weakness as well as in its strength. The humor shows, not the counsel of despair to warm one's hands before a dying fire (although the Wife feels something of the sort), but an expansive and, as we have seen, characteristic belief in life.

I may take as an example the marvellous commentary the Wife gives on the story of the Samaritan woman. Our Lord has told the woman:

> "Thou hast yhad fyve housbondes," quod He,
> "And that ilke man that now hath thee
> Is noght thyn housbonde" . . .
>   D. 17-19.

The Wife is enormously puzzled. Why wasn't the fifth man a husband? It worries her because she herself has had five. There is a kind of humility as well as daring in the tone of what she says:

> What that He mente therby, I kan nat seyn;
> But that I axe, why that the fifthe man
> Was noon housbonde to the Samaritan?
> How manye myghte she have in mariage?
> Yet herde I nevere tellen in myn age
> Upon this nombre diffinicioun.
>   D. 20-25.

I wish I might have been present when Chaucer thought of this wonderful poser for the Wife of Bath. To have seen his face and heard his laugh would have been to catch some of the finest essence of his personality. What a great idea it is, and how rich is the picture of the good Wife fussing about this blunder! Our joy in it, however, is not in any picture of the breakdown of a character attempting to furbish up an excuse for sexual indulgence. It must be remembered that the Wife's *joie de vivre* in itself is a good thing as far as it goes, not as a matter of self-interest but as an expression of positive vitality.

Anyone makes a great mistake who thinks that the poet jeers at virginity when he makes the Wife say:

> The dart is set up for virginitee:
> Cacche whoso may, who renneth best lat see.
>
> D. 75–76.

He may well enjoy the humor of the idea that few will seek that prize, but that is another matter. We can see this point quite clearly further along when he writes (and the Wife says):

> Virginitee is greet perfeccion,
> And continence eek with devocion,
> But Crist, that of perfeccion is welle,
> Bad nat every wight he sholde go selle
> Al that he hadde, and gyve it to the poore
> And in swich wise folwe hym and his foore.
>
> D. 105–110.

The logic is delightful; it is also unassailable. The poet does not here launch an attack against virginity and Christian charity as well. And we miss the full meaning of the portrait of the Wife if we suppose that the poet heartily agreed with her at every turn: where she placed her emphasis and how she allowed her sophistry to function in her own behalf. If she is a heroine preaching emancipated views which her auditors (and Chaucer's) were really meant to adopt, then she is not half so funny as I find her. The superb garment of her humor vanishes, and she seems to me a rather meager prophet. Do we hear the poet's voice in the Wife's words saying, "Come, my children, listen to what I really have to tell you. Often and often I have rung the schoolbell to summon you to moral and spiritual instruction. But that was just a pose. Here before you in this good Wife is the heart of life. Take your fun as she does. Live your lives high, wide, and handsome; for that is all that is really left to us!" Neither the hypocrisy involved here nor the appeal sounds in the least like Chaucer. Moreover it entirely misses the spirit of this glorious Prologue.

The Wife takes pleasure in a rather excessive use of words that were not often spoken (even in the fourteenth century) in mixed company. Her euphemisms are not effective as such in the least; their quality lies in the fact that they conceal nothing but, on the contrary, frame the unmentionable with rococo delight. Are we to think that the poet himself took the same childish satisfaction in the bawdy? Perhaps we can more accurately guess at the date of his birth by assuming that it was a dangerous age for him when he began reading Deschamps's *Miroir de Mariage*! The Wife of Bath is far less a miraculous creation if she is the embodiment in all these details of what Chaucer believed in at this time. Of course, the fact is that he sees all around her; he detects her pleasure in exhibitionism even to the degree of her reference to the mark of Mars "in another privee place." He knows intuitively the satisfaction she gets from suggestive language, as when she tells how she described her dream of the blood-filled bed to the attractive young clerk. Incidentally here we can see the perfect drama involved, in which Chaucer is spectator as well as creator; for the Wife obviously gets so excited with recalling her narrative of that foul dream that she forgets what comes next.

> But now, sire, lat me se, what shal I seyn?
> A ha! by God, I have my tale ageyn.
> D. 585–586.

Are we to suppose that Chaucer too was so moved that he lost track of the sequence?

But perhaps we are only to think that Chaucer's obvious liking of the Wife of Bath spells fundamental cynicism. The problem is like that of his description of the first union of Troilus and Criseyde. As artist he seems to approve of what he describes so supremely well. I think, as I have said, he enjoyed the spectacle of Troilus's winning Cressid, and as far as it goes relished the beauty of that first night. But all this could not disturb his moral judgment. So too I feel no doubt that Chaucer enormously liked the Wife of Bath, and I think M. Cazamian goes far astray when he speaks of "the cruelty that lives at the heart of her selfishness." It is, however, the depth of absurdity to suppose that for Chaucer she represented the fully admirable any more than she did the fully desirable, just as it is foolish to think that young Troilus sitting in a gloom and kicking about fate is the poet's own mouthpiece and prophet. Shakespeare found great zest, no doubt, in the creation of Falstaff; but he also wrote "I know thee not, old man. Fall to thy prayers."

We have some reason to think that what is now the *Shipman's Tale* was originally assigned to the Wife of Bath. If such was the case, we find little difference in the lady who had that story, except that her delight in cheating is later replaced by her interest in *maistrye*. What a fine counterpart the account of Dan John made for the *Franklin's Tale*, in what was perhaps an earlier Marriage Cycle! The wife's eager adultery, and the fact that both husband and wife pay the penalty of the hundred franks, stand in contrast to Dorigen's modesty and the general remitting of the debt according to the Franklin's plot. But even in what the Shipman tells, where self-interest flourishes, there is no implication that such is the whole of life and such all humanity. It is just a fabliau, and far weaker in characterization than the more optimistic *Franklin's Tale*. We cannot justly infer cynicism from the ordinary run of risqué stories: they show people beguiled by tricks that are sometimes dirty and sometimes also amusing. But, as the Reeve concludes his narrative: "A gylour shal hymself bigyled be" (A. 4321), and there is no gospel of cynicism in that! Chaucer has many rogues who cheat and lie and live on the fleshpots of their day; but the Wife of Bath is far better than most. If she does not discriminate she has at least a generous spirit.

But what of the flavor of the story told by the embittered Merchant? When it does not pause for sarcasm it makes room for dramatic irony. Sarcasm appears in such lines as:

A wyf is Goddes yifte verraily;
Alle othere manere yiftes hardily,

> As londes, rentes, pasture, or commune,
> Or moebles, alle been yiftes of Fortune,
> That passen as a shadwe upon a wal.
> But drede nat, if pleynly speke I shal,
> A wyf wol laste, and in thyn hous endure,
> Wel lenger than thee list, paraventure.
>   E. 1311-1318.

The withered old January wants his sensation, the shallow May will have her fun, and there is no one here who spends much time thinking about idealism. Even the gods above (or at least the fairies) are occupied with the earthy problem, and Proserpine has nothing but sympathy for the heroine. January's speech to his wife is heavy with irony:

> "Beth to me trewe, and I wol telle yow why.
> Thre thynges, certes, shal ye wynne therby:
> First, love of Crist, and to youreself honour,
> And al myn heritage, toun and tour."
>   E. 2169-2172.

Here, if you will, is cynicism, and aplenty. But it is not borne out by the general mood of the Marriage Cycle. It stands in such violent contrast to the rest of the poetry that its harshness has struck everybody, and the Merchant's grief thus expressed has received ample comment. But this cynicism, far from representing all of Chaucer, does not even represent all of the Merchant. It stands in contrast with his belief in life in general now frustrated and poisoned by his own recent experience in wedlock. The violence in mood he shows when he says of his own lady "She is a shrewe at al" reveals a conflict with what he has known of happiness elsewhere and with what he thinks life can yield.

A real cynic can hardly become turbulent; if he is surprised enough at life to become excited he gives away his game. Moreover, if this bitter satire is meant to register a permanent effect upon us, Chaucer did poorly to follow it with the charm and freshness of the *Squire's Tale*. More than that, because of its greater realism, he also spoiled the effect by ending the cycle with the *Franklin's Tale*. Perhaps I should add that I am not among those who would move this latter story elsewhere or ignore the obvious and varied ties that bind together this closely knit set of stories treating of the themes of marriage, gentilesse, rhetoric, and other matters. More than all this Chaucer spoiled the effect of his cynicism (if that is what he wanted to gain) by the introductory speech of the Wife of Bath, with her abundant faith and joy tainted with few negatives.

Let us with relief return to her. One important moral of her proem, I take it, is that she holds not worth a leek the mouse that has only one hole to escape to. There, if you will, is self-interest and a pretty humdrum view of human nature. But are we to suppose that what Chaucer liked here was the evidence that the Wife wasn't taken in by much; that she knew her way about; that at the funeral of one husband she was sizing up the ankles of a man who might prove to be another mate for her? Well, perhaps! But with all her resourcefulness the Wife does not always succeed; exasperation is a note of her Prologue quite as often as triumph. The truth is that critics are likely to see Chaucer's admiration where their own approval falls. Catholics will look for proof that the poet was loyal to his religion; moderns will try to see in him that shrewd eye which they think to find in modern disillusionment. If the critic himself rejoices in cynicism, then he will be eager to find the poet turning more and more cynical as the years advance, because it is gratifying to discover that a genius has as much good sense as oneself. But I find really no evidence that Chaucer turned cynical. In this I may myself end on a naïvely romantic note because I am eager to find just this conclusion; cynicism is not a mark of greatness, and Chaucer is great. I insist that there is ample evidence that he was not touched with this disease, evidence in the many disturbing signs of optimism and faith and general health of outlook in the poet.

A cynic's laugh, I should imagine, must be bitter. What might give him joy in seeing life on its lowest terms would be either an egoistic satisfaction at not being fooled himself and at seeing others fooled, or possibly a fine serenity based on the consciousness that one could hardly be surprised at any pitfalls again. But neither emotion, I think, could serve to provide a happy laughter which contains an element of hope. This, I may say, is what I hear in Chaucer's poetry over and over again. The realist is not depressed as he goes on. The portrait of the Wife of Bath, done in Chaucer's maturity, shows less of a spiritual person than that of Blanche the Duchess, done in his "youthe." That is true enough. But by the time the Wife came lunging on horseback over the horizon, the poet had also created the Prioress, and had thought considerably of the virtues of the Plowman and the Parson. There is, for all I have said on the subject in earlier chapters, a kind of mysticism in the *Canterbury Tales*. It is not primarily in thoughts of the shrine toward which the pilgrims are moving. It is a little expressed in certain exalted passages like the lines based on St Bernard's prayer. It is found in the sufferings of characters like Constance and Griselda and Virginia, who, it is exceedingly important to note, are not sentimental heroines destroyed by overwhelming fate but willing victims and so in their way saintly. But most of all it is found in the hearty belief in human nature that comes out in the positive and sunny humor surrounding even Nicholas and Alisoun, the Wife of Bath and the naughty Friar. Where we find torture as with the Merchant and the Pardoner, the exception tests the rule. Even here, however, the violent negative is not always emphasized and it sets off the positive elsewhere in relief.

We may see Chaucer's development through the various periods of his life less, I think, in terms of an occasional lapse into this mood or that, whether naïf, sentimental, sophisticated or cynical, than in a perceptible flowering and enrichment of talents he seems to have possessed at the outset. In the various types that come to Fame asking for one reward or another there is an expression of what by itself might be regarded as cynicism. For instance there is the group of idle wretches who nevertheless want (and obtain) an undeserved reputation. If we should isolate that part of the story we might say that it showed the poet in a state of sad disillusionment. In the *Parliament* there is the black inscription of the gate of Love. But such passages are balanced by others, and the total effect is that which implies a poet of a rounded and well-endowed personality. There is the hopeful humor of the *Book of the Duchess*, a mood that in different ways continues in the other early works and prevails even in the background of *Troilus and Criseyde*. This too is found in his later poems, the same spirit of detachment and sense of proportion and sane amusement, not destructive and pessimistic but with a kind of healthy promise in it (as with Fielding's satire) that life will be found good. This is really what we have, I think, all through the Wife of Bath's Prologue as well as in her story. It gives an impression of well-being and essential soundness. Nowhere does it suggest the disruption of moral principles or any exposure of their failure. For all through Chaucer's poetry, however much these may be violated by the characters, we have the abiding certainty that such principles are ingrained in the fabric of life itself. May's successful venture in the garden does not ultimately convey the idea that the world is safe for immorality. May, the Wife of Bath, Alisoun, and the others of this type, appear for what they really are against the general background of the world and experience, the sum total of which serves mercilessly to reveal their shortcomings. The poet had no reason to worry about the stories that "sownen into synne."

If he had indeed been tempted to cynicism he would have had less faith than he seems to have had in marriage. What is love, another poet asks: 'tis not hereafter! But all through Chaucer's works there is a fairly steady loyalty to the idea of the benediction of wedded love: in the case of Blanche the Duchess; in the *House of Fame* and the *Parliament*, I think; even the *Man of Law's Tale*, the story of Griselda, the Melibeus, the *Nun's Priest's Tale* (I insist on this), the *Second Nun's Tale*, and the *Franklin's Tale*. Where husbands or wives are cheated, there is no apparent implication that the Sacrament of Matrimony is itself at fault. Even in the *Merchant's Tale*, where we have echoes of the marriage ceremony and

ironic passages on the subject of wedded bliss, the idea that
by marriage one renders licentiousness legal and sexual self-
indulgence moral is exposed to ruthless satire. Old January
explains his conduct thus:

> "I have my body folily despended;
> Blessed be God that it shal been amended!
> For I wol be, certeyn, a wedded man,
> And that anoon in al the haste I kan."
>
> E. 1403–1406.

Such is Chaucer's comment on the idea that wedlock rectifies
loose-living; such his respect for marriage itself. But his
ideas of love are more inclusive than the question of such
attachments. A rather pretty essay can some day be written
by anyone who will consult and analyze the many uses of
the word "love" in the Concordance of the poet's works. It
occupies about as much space, in proportion to the modest
amount in general allowed to other words, as the Wife
of Bath herself among the pilgrims. It has chiefly to do
(I think, though I have not counted the instances) with the
kind of love that the Wife and Sir Thopas and Palamon and
Dorigen and the rest are occupied with. But there is also
reference to the "love of God" and "God's love" and not
merely as an oath. Incidentally I am rather fascinated by the
Concordance. I note that for one reason or another "God"
occupies still more space than "love." Oaths here again con-
tribute much; I have not yet counted how much. But even
oaths, like hypocrisy, are a tribute to virtue.

In Chaucer there is love of people, love of places, love of
books and much else. The world of his experience is full of
it. Love of God is there too —

And loveth hym, the which that right for love
Upon a crois, oure soules for to beye,
First starf, and roos, and sit in hevene above.
Troilus and Criseyde, v, 1842–1844.

The first thought that came to him here is that Christ died
for love. Love for Our Lady is what moves the little Clergeoun quite as much as it is love for the yet unknown *amie*
that spurs Thopas to his task. "For soothly the lawe of God is
the love of God," says the Parson finely in his disquisition
(I, 125), echoing the pseudo-Dionysius. But there is a vast
amount, here and there in Chaucer's works, about love of
people. It is in the poet himself. It is what stirs him as he talks
about the young Squire's embroidered garb, the Clerk's
twenty books, the Prioress's little dogs and her nonsense
about them, the Plowman and his excellent load of manure,
and all the rest of it. His characters are all the best of their
kind; that point has been noticed elsewhere by a great critic.
The tendency thus to display them could have been taken
over from medieval romance, where the same thing pretty
well holds true, and also from the poet's own taste for finish
and perfection. But it also springs from the fact that he has an
undoubted love for all his characters, all but one, and even
there he concedes as much as he can bear to. The Pardoner
is a clever rascal.

This love I speak of is no sentimental imagining. It is
clearer at some times than at others, notably with the Plowman and the Franklin and the Wife of Bath. If we must be
temperate we may describe it as a kindly attitude. But that
is not enough. It has been perceived by many critics, and is
referred to in such phrases as "sympathetic irony," "not un-

kindly cynicism," "gentle" or "genial Chaucer." If we contrast his characterizations with those that appear in other
writers, say Froissart or Deschamps or Boccaccio, the difference (apart from the mere question of a fuller realism) is at
once apparent. A kind of personal relationship seems to
exist between the English poet and the *dramatis personae* of
his narratives. He often adds to his portraits a touch of what
is (or certainly seems to be) a personal estimate. He would
excuse Criseyde if he could. It was "a verray, parfit, gentil
knyght." Of the Doctor, "In al this world ne was ther noon
hym lik." "A bettre preest I trowe that nowher noon ys." Of
the Manciple:

> Now is nat that of God a ful fair grace
> That swich a lewed mannes wit shal pace
> The wisdom of an heep of lerned men?
> A. 573–575.

Of the Summoner, "A bettre felawe sholde men noght
fynde." And so on, and so on. Chaucer loves human nature;
yes, but he loves the individual Tom and Dick and Harry —
in varying degree, no doubt, but in reality. Moreover I find
this kindly attitude steadily marked by that sense of proportion which is humor. And the outlook here revealed in the
poet shows a positive element of belief and confidence so
marked that I would call it mystical. A slight touch of that
appears, for example, when more from affection than for didacticism he does his pilgrims more than justice: of the
Clerk, "Noght o word spak he moore than was neede"; of
the Parson, "That first he wroghte, and afterward he
taughte"; of the Knight, "He nevere yet no vileynye ne

sayde." Such lines, challenging exceptions as they do, suggest a complimentary glance rather than realistic portrayal.

The tone and temper of all this art is poles removed from anything that we may justly call cynical. If it is, on the other hand more nearly naïf, it is naïf only as trusting friendship, candor, belief in God, may be so described. Rather it is clear and fresh and unspoiled, like sunlight early in the morning when the day has not been used. We have only to compare the poet's work with that of Swift or Byron to see how absurd the charge of cynicism really is. As well call Browning a cynic because of his poem *The Bishop Orders his Tomb*, or *Mr. Sludge*, or *Bishop Blougram's Apology*. The man who wrote, "Lo! 'Lieth flat, and loveth Setebos!" *must* be a cynic! Chaucer is not irresponsible when it comes to philosophy or morals or religion. But dominant in his spirit I find — among other things — a leaning toward fun, which to the naïvely romantic may seem cynical, and, on the other hand, to the cynical it probably seems naïvely romantic. When he was young he should have been sentimental and romantic and weak; but he was not. Humor saved him. With a fuller view of humanity, with certain disillusionments no doubt, he should have become embittered; but he did not. Humor again saved him — or a healthy mind, or kindliness, or whatever it is we all find irresistible in the man.

INDEX

INDEX